A CALL TO GOD

James Ellis is a writer and independent researcher from the UK. He is the author of four other books including *Only Ever Freedom and Be Not Afraid*. He is also the host of the Hermitix Podcast.

A CALL TO GOD
A Spiritual Introduction to Christianity

James Ellis

AEON

First published in 2024 by
Aeon Books

Copyright © 2024 by James Ellis

The right of James Ellis to be identified as the author of this work has been asserted in accordance with §§ 77 and 78 of the Copyright Design and Patents Act 1988.

All rights reserved. No part of this publication may be reproduced, stored in a retrieval system, or transmitted, in any form or by any means, electronic, mechanical, photocopying, recording, or otherwise, without the prior written permission of the publisher.

British Library Cataloguing in Publication Data

A C.I.P. for this book is available from the British Library

ISBN-13: 978-1-80152-105-5

Typeset by Medlar Publishing Solutions Pvt Ltd, India

www.aeonbooks.co.uk

*Dedicated to Naomi, Gerry, Shaun, Judith,
Steve, Judi, and Adam*

CONTENTS

INTRODUCTION ix

PART 1: THE CHRISTIAN IN THE MODERN WORLD
My turbulent journey 3
    The modern world 7
    The soul in the modern world 12
    The Reformation, the sacred, and Couliano 16
    Alternative spiritual currents 18
What Christianity isn't 21
What Christianity is 29
The Old and New Testaments 35
The Life of Christ 37
The passion 57
The Sacraments 61
The soul 65
The afterlife 69

PART 2: THE PATH OF THE CHRISTIAN

Grace	79
Love	89
Faith	97
Humility and silence	109
Seeds	121
Rich and poor	131
Light and darkness	141
Will	147
The afterlife, salvation, and a possible conclusion	159
BIBLIOGRAPHY	163
INDEX	165

INTRODUCTION

As is usually the case with introductions, it took me until completing this book to be able to write this one. It's not until one has at least an abstract sense of the whole that they can begin to declare what they intend to do with the parts. This is another book about Christianity, another book introducing Christianity. It's from the point of view of someone who was for a long time an atheist, someone living amidst modernity, and someone who struggles with dogma. It's for these reasons that the subtitle of this book is specifically 'a *spiritual* introduction to Christianity'; for so many wish to describe Christianity by leaping to the end without ever giving thought to just how it is we get there. When we think about Christianity we might think about hell, heaven, judgement, and 'thou shalt nots', all the while also thinking to ourselves 'Slow down, I'm still living for goodness sake!'

It's only now I can state that what I attempt to achieve here is a spiritual approach to Christianity that practically reverses the Trinity. We have all heard of the Trinity, of 'The Father, the Son, and the Holy Spirit', and it is in that order that we almost always approach the Trinity, with the Father first, the Son second, and the Holy Spirit last. Theologically speaking, this is the correct order of manifestation and creation. Yet, there is a descension from above, down from the Father, mediated by the Son, and brought into ourselves as the Holy Spirit. So, from the point of view of us humble humans here on earth, if we are to approach the Trinity (God) in this manner, we attempt to understand the conclusion before undertaking the journey. We seek to grasp the rules, laws, and commandments of the Father before feeling His presence within us. Underlying the book that follows, then, I seek to approach God with the Trinity reversed, for as it emanated and descended down to earth, we need to follow it back upward towards the Light. That is, the Holy Spirit, to the Son, and then to the Father. We need to feel close to God in an emphatically (Holy) *spiritual* sense first before we can even begin to think of such things as Jesus Christ the Son of God or God the Father, for if we haven't that quiet experience within ourselves first what are we doing but heading blindly into something we *wish* would be?

We begin to feel there is *something more,* this is then mediated through *the* mediator that was and is Jesus Christ and His teachings, and from this we can begin to understand the full picture of God as the fount of all being. It is rare for one to state that perhaps the best place to begin is not with a church but with oneself, but I feel that if it is the case that one never had an experience of God to begin with, what can anything down the line be except ignorant fideism?

This book is about the *journey* and not the end, the *spirit* and not the dogma. As such, it's split roughly into two parts. The first half details my own journey, the modern mindset we bring with us that blocks the Spirit out, the basics of the language of Christianity without any fluff attached, and simple places to begin one's journey. The second half investigates the deeper themes of Christianity whilst attempting to always draw them back to practical, everyday use.

Throughout this book, there are ten very simple exercises one can use to get in touch with the Spirit. Not in any psychic or magical sense, but prayerfully and physically by being here in the world and trying to look at it through new eyes. One can disregard these exercises if they wish and read this as a simple textual introduction, one could read up to each exercise and then spend a few days sitting with the results, or one could even just do the exercises. Either way, I feel that an approach to Christianity that doesn't begin with the Spirit, that is, personal experience of God, is lopsided and tends only to control people.

I hope this book brings you peace, joy, and love.

PART 1

THE CHRISTIAN IN THE MODERN WORLD

My turbulent journey

Before I truly get to the heart of Christian spirituality and try to answer the question of what exactly Christianity *is*, I feel the need to give some minor exposition on my own journey. I don't consider my call or journey to God special or in any sense unique. Perhaps the one thing that slightly sets it apart from other conversions is that it is relatively recent. I found God around 2020, officially converted to Catholicism in Easter of 2022, and then the journey *really* began in early 2023. The slow process of being guided by the Lord's light took roughly three years. So, unlike other popular conversion stories, mine is not set in the past (unless you're reading this in 2100 …), it is a conversion that took place amidst the confusion, disorientation, and palpable nihilism of the modern world. I speak here, then, of conversion in its broadest sense, a movement from the constraints of secular modernity to the openness of God and the Divine.

The reason I think it is important to mention my own journey is that I come from a notably average background, and, from those who I have spoken to, a background that is increasingly common. When I was very young I went to a (so-called) Church of England school. I say 'so-called' because, in retrospect, all sincerely religious elements were left out, leaving me with a perspective of Christianity that was entirely false. I said the Lord's Prayer, and we performed a Harvest festival ... and that was about it in terms of spirituality—at the time none of us were educated as to the actual importance of these things. This is to say that in my early years, Christianity was for me just another institution, it had been stripped of its divine elements, and strewn amidst the world as nothing other than a didactic tool. As I stated in the introduction, what happened here was that the physical institution, dogma, and rules came *before* the spirituality, therein leading to a fatal imbalance, for the former makes zero internal sense without the latter.

This early pseudo-religious education quickly led me away from belief in God, but as is the case with any human being I of course still craved meaning and purpose. And so I quickly filled the God-shaped-hole in my heart with the offerings of the modern world—jobs, money, things, consumerism, alcohol, drugs, sex, etc. At the same time, I was quickly becoming interested in reading and ideas. Armed, however, with the faux-Christianity I had been taught in my childhood, my appreciation of many concepts and ideas was crippled by my neglect of theology, casting the entirety of Christianity into the common bin of 'fairy tales' and nonsense as so many moderns do. As will come as no surprise, an interest in ideas and a subtle scorn for religion within the 2000s could only lead a young person to one destination, New Atheism.

Around the age of 15, I began to consume the writings of Hitchens, Harris, and Dawkins as quickly as I could. They were my intellectual idols at that point in time, and their—largely *ad hominem*—attacks on religion served as a replacement for religion itself. Prolonged avoidance of actually *constructing* meaning in one's life is quite easy when you believe you are correct, such a sense of intellectual superiority can carry you for quite a while, but eventually, as with all material things, that also falters. As I proceeded through my years of education I remained fervently an atheist-materialist, eventually heading into the retrospectively obvious conclusion of nihilism, and therein falling out the other side of university something like an intellectually arrogant, spiritually bereft, cynical alcoholic. Any semblance of meaning I found in my life at this juncture came from the general understanding that God was dead and only those who admitted this were right, anyone else was just holding a pretence to keep themselves from going mad. Of course, unapparent to me at the time was the fact that just because you feel you have proved a statement incorrect doesn't inherently mean your criticism applied a new solution. Deconstruction and critique only last so long before anything and everything is fodder for one's cynical ruin.

And yet, as the years went on, all I saw was the world go mad. As nihilism—veiled in the language of hedonistic consumerism—accelerated itself into becoming a modern virtue, I perceived the world become more depressed and anxious, more beholden to things than people, less able to discern right from wrong, and generally speaking, more prideful, greedy, and sensual. The world seemed to be—and still is—having a prolonged panic attack. Stripped of the One which holds it in existence, modernity shrieks and gasps as it hastily seeks the next alternative for God; modernity is an eternal lack, a desire never fulfilled, a peace never found.

In begrudgingly seeing this as a failure of the ideas I had come to treasure so dear, I headed towards the other common path of meaning with the modern world, alternative religions and spiritualities. I acquired the general feeling of *the* lack which is articulated within the modern world within the oft-repeated question: 'There must be more to life than this?' But of course, armed only with the tepid and incorrect form of Christianity most of us are badly taught, it was out of the question for me to return to Christ at that juncture. However, I did think that maybe there is something *else* out there, perhaps there is something to be found deep in my unconscious mind or at the end of a long meditation session. At this point this was all relatively easy to subsume into the materialist framework, such practices were little more than tools to appease the hunger in my soul for a little while longer.

In terms of the other currents and paths I actually followed, that's a long story that doesn't need telling in full here, but I made my way through quite a few, picking up pieces of truth and peace here and there, but never feeling at home, never understanding in the depths of my being that I touched upon the root of Truth itself. At this juncture, many might state something like 'As *luck* would have it!' or 'Lucky for me!', but what happened at this point had nothing to do with luck and everything to do with God. Quite simply, I began to pray. Specifically, a form of prayer called 'open prayer', where one simply sits and opens themselves to God.

Some might also state that the previous time spent flirting with other mystical paths led me to pray, some could consider it a matter of submission, or many might contend that it was merely an act of desperation. I would state, with the clarity of hindsight, that it was none of these things. It was likely grace, but this isn't easily defined due to its experiential nature. This is the reason why, however, in Part 2, I place grace before all other themes. Grace comes first, and, as defined by the Catechism of the Catholic Church, 'grace is favour, the free and undeserved help that God gives us to respond to his call to become children of God, adoptive sons, partakers of the divine nature and of eternal life' (*Catechism of the Catholic Church*, 1995)—I was, then, amidst the turbulence, disorientation, and darkness of modern nihilism, given a *choice*—Do I accept God, the Divine, and the possibility there is Spirit? Or do I shrug such help off as some-or-other psychological phenomenon? There was no way I could do such a thing, for God is … different.

However, very few paths are stable and straightforward, and as satisfying as it would be to simply state that I found a single path to be without its ups and downs, this wouldn't be entirely true. It is true that I went through catechesis for one year and was then Baptised and confirmed Catholic in April of 2022. I then threw myself into Catholic life with a fervour I'd never found before. For a while, it held fast and I was on a singular path up the mountain. Yet, there is a reason I entitled this first section 'My *Turbulent* Journey' because that path is still admittedly rocky. Sometimes I feel I can't make the leaps needed of me, sometimes I don't feel I can't step foot in church, when other times I'm ready to stride through the doors. Sometimes the Voice is loud and other times it's quiet. From the outside, so many individual journeys seem stable and secure, as if once the path had been chosen it was simply a case of walking straight forward and not looking back. I'm here to say that the path is difficult. Being a Christian is hard work. You might personally find your own journey to be easy, difficult, confusing, exhausting, or even exhilarating; whatever it is, stick with it and try to hold onto that gentle Voice that brought you onto the path in the first place. Equally, do not fret or chastise yourself if the path you thought set out for you didn't work, that inner voice will be with you whatever happens and will remain throughout your individual journey up the mountain.

This note brings us to the present day, wherein God, the Absolute, the Divine—whatever name one prefers—has become both more complex and more simple all at once, and what's left is to follow the trail where it leads and try to grow as you do. Personally, I feel it's a message— there is not a single path to God—that one can refuse to learn (by way of armouring themselves against contradictions), learn the hard way (coming up against themselves), or the easy way (by being loving).

Either way, I'm happy to share and admit to the turbulence and doubt that has accompanied me on my journey here as a means to say that it will work out, take your time, and don't stress too much. In finding yourself in a situation where your relationship with God has become one solely of terror, worry, and guilt, perhaps it's time to take a step back and ease off. In my opinion, this certainly isn't love and one needs to withdraw and get back to basics of what it is simply to believe and love in that *something more* one sought after for so long.

For now, you only need to know this about me—I was once a 'normal', everyday, modern atheist-materialist. Some days I loathed God, others I laughed at Him, but mostly I just shrugged Him off. And now? Now I am a Seeker who is with Christ. I will go where I'm needed and open myself to where the path takes me.

The modern world

Following on from my own journey, and before we get to Christianity proper, I want to investigate the world within which that journey took place. The so-called 'modern world'. Before we can even begin to understand Christianity (or any sacred system for that matter) we need to at least try to understand just what it is *we* are mentally—and often physically—bringing to the table. What presumptions, habits, and errors do our default worldview hold that might make approaching Christ a difficult task? What is it that we presumptively hold that may make our understanding of certain traditions and religions not just difficult, but actually impossible?

Christ is an afterthought within contemporary society. Christianity is a crucifix necklace, a dated belief system, an oppressive institution, or simply another story among others which one might choose from to define themselves. The modern world is all about choice and individuality, and so it's no surprise that a single God who upholds all individual wills is a bit difficult to swallow for modern men and women. With this said, if Christianity—and being a Christian—is to be taken seriously (both by society and the Christians themselves) then it cannot be anything other than the foundation from which we understand all things. It is not the case that one can be a Christian *some* of the time—we either are or aren't, and if we are to be Christians, then *everything* changes. This form of an absolute worldview goes against some of the key prime directives of modernity, namely: choice, flexibility, and freedom.

Having to adhere to a worldview that applies *all* of the time is inherently incompatible with the general emancipative attitude of the moderns. But what differentiates the Christian form of faith from modern choice is that the former is understood to arrive from elsewhere (not from ourselves) and so it isn't our choice to make.

So the key problem here is that the modern world abhors foundations, it dislikes rules and detests limitations. If something can be 'emancipated' within modernity then due to the very fact it *isn't* free it is therefore understood as something that *should* be. Rarely do we question whether certain limitations are good. But this form of thinking—of limitation and limit—is itself, ironically, inherently modern. The idea that a definite selection of choices will result in perfect, individual outcomes is emphatically a trait of *progress*. The *myth* of progress therein is that we just need to make the 'correct' choices to continue progressing towards an ever-greater future, despite such a future is impossible for a variety of reasons, most clearly the fact that there is no agreed-upon notion of just where it is we are heading. The myth of progress—the underlying myth and God of modern times—is free-floating, it doesn't adhere to anything and yet can be summoned in defence of any spontaneous whim. However, trade-offs don't just exist, they are part and parcel of what it even is to exist. So from this basis, let's not waste any time and look at the common reasons why one is ignorant of Christianity and *being* Christian in the modern world.

First there is the clearest case that one doesn't believe in God (the name 'God' is something I will get to very soon). In such a case, as we shall see when we get to the sections on grace and faith, this is a belief that is primarily (if not entirely) between God and the individual themselves. This isn't to say there's nothing other people or the world can do to influence someone's belief in God, only that it is solely God and each individual alone who knows the Truth in their heart. One might persuade someone to come to church week after week or recite prayers night after night, but it is up to the Grace of God to instil genuine faith within their heart. Following this, I need to emphasise that this isn't a book of apologetics, I am not here to *prove* the existence of God. Besides, anyone who has spent a fair amount of time within that selection of debates will understand that such a thing can never be done in a solely intellectual or worldly sense. This is to say, not once have I seen either side of a debate sway the other side toward their viewpoint. Maybe this is because humans are very pig-headed. Maybe it's because of sunk costs. Or maybe it's because debates are made up of words and not actions. I don't know. All I know is that 99% of the time debate, defence, and attack just waste energy that could *actually* be used for Good.

Second, and seemingly more honestly, there is the fact that being a Christian within the modern world is understood as a severe limitation to one's possible freedoms. It's *very* easy to ignore God and religion in general if one *already* holds the view that it will only limit their life. First and (almost always) foremost is the fact one needs to wait until marriage to have sex, then there is charity and time given up for others, and of course there is the apparently dull and dry affair of having to go to Church every Sunday morning. Everything about Christianity's supposedly apparent archaisms appears dated and contrary to all we've been led to believe is good. Relating this back to the introduction, this is another case wherein the morality of Christianity overtakes and suffocates everything else. When most people think of Christianity they think of rules and laws, not love, kindness, and a relationship with God. This is all backwards. The ignorantly pernicious education regarding Christianity (and many other religions) from modern schooling conflates the entirety of belief solely with morals, thereby making many people believe that searching for God will only result in a hindrance. It's rare to see people freely discuss what being a Christian might afford their life as opposed to what it might seemingly take away. This kind of conversation revolves around modern choice and modern freedom, 'Ah, you want me to do something, well, what's in it for me and what are the costs?' See, modern man just wants to keep going forwards, he wants to keep progressing, even though we've been progressing for quite some time now and things appear to be more chaotic than ever.

The problem is that the modern world revolves around a sense of freedom which is always positive. Freedom, for the 'moderns', is always the freedom *of* or *for*: freedom of choice, of place, of gender, of style, of taste, and freedom for more, for X, or for Y. In short, modern man's freedom is always based on the presumption that consumption, addition, and excess are synonymous with better, freer, or more progressive. To enact his freedom modern man needs to acquire, consume, show, tell, or display. His personal freedom is always aggrandising. His freedom builds upon itself like a cancer until his freedom becomes so top-heavy he finds he has to develop a new form of positive freedom to thus decrease his previous freedom, thus always remaining in the bounds of more, more, more. For instance, many contemporary forms of simplicity and minimalism have become so detached from their original definitions that they have become habits of addition and not subtraction. We see this in the notion of minimalist aesthetics, whereby one still owns the same amount of objects but they're all white or grey. Thus, even the freedom to not have something becomes a consumptive freedom. One doesn't simply adhere to simple living, one consumes the 'simple living' lifestyle. One might even go so far as to say that certain people may even end up consuming the Christian 'lifestyle', adhering to an aesthetic sense of piety and wholesomeness as a means to give off a distinct impression to neighbours, in spite of the fact the *internal* values that should naturally lead to that *externality* are not there at all. This is a case of mistaking word for Word, something I will also get to later.

Christianity, and what it means to *be* a Christian, in part, is to develop an understanding of freedom which grows—as a seed—from an acceptance and understanding of God's Will, that is to say, a higher calling arrived at via prayer, contemplation, and love. There is no such thing as pure freedom or pure individuality. We, as human beings and as singular men and women, are beholden to the foundations, rules, and laws of creation and its Creator. Or, if you prefer the name 'Absolute' instead of 'God', we are beholden to universal limitations regarding our innate being and how we live. For believers, this is God's law, from which comes an understanding of Natural Law and the ways things are meant to be. One begins to notice that as they push against God's Will, in a futile attempt at personal freedom, the freedom they acquire is tainted, uncanny, and never quite satisfactory. Let's take for instance, once again, the most modern of freedoms, sex. Our newfound social freedom (via the advent of contraception and various other technologies) has allowed men and women alike to have sex with who they like when they like, and as much as they like, without the prior natural consequences (birth, which once upon a time would also mean marriage). We appear to collectively understand this 'emancipation' as only a good thing, all the while ignoring the consequences of *this* freedom wherein sex (pleasure) becomes an end for its own sake; the central focus of many lives becomes solely the pursuit of minute, temporary pleasures. In time this freedom has not led to a greater sense of well-being, but increased societal loneliness, alienation, and a growing appreciation of sex that is focused almost solely on the physical climax as opposed to closeness, affection, and love. This is just one case, I am sure you the reader can draw out the equal trade-offs found within our modern relationships with, say, food, travel, and wealth as further examples.

Perhaps it is the case that the person reading this understands many newfound freedoms of the modern world to be a good thing. That's fine, I'm not here to try to fit everyone into a strait jacket. It's only that there is always a trade-off and modernity seeks to ignore this point. One may, to use the language of Christianity, be gluttonous but one will also become physically unhealthy. One may decide to be lustful and sleep around, yet in time find they possibly struggle to connect to others. One may be greedy and try to scoop up all the wealth they can, finding near the end that life has passed them by and not a single penny will follow them to the grave. Individuals make decisions based on their own beliefs, but there is always a polarity and always some consequence. Now, no religion is going to make a choice *for* you—in fact, it can't, as your heart and body know the score—but it will, if understood correctly, allow one a mirror to perceive a higher, more holistic and wholesome view of their purpose in this life.

The modern mindset brings with it inherent disbelief (based on materialist assumptions), a fear of limitation (based on presumed perfect freedom), and finally an external denial of death and suffering (mortality). I emphasise an *external* denial of mortality because internally it is something we can never deny nor even ignore. Of all the supposed truths of life, there is but one of which all are certain, namely, death. Now it need not be a morbid fixation, nor do we need to be scared of it (as we shall see in the next section), but in relation to faith, death becomes something entirely different, especially when compared with its modern appreciation. See, in daily modern life, we speak of illness and suffering in hushed tones, acknowledging it as strictly a differentiation from the norm, that which should not be. Likewise, we perform much the same operation with death except this time we do so with far more enthusiasm. Death is outsourced to hospitals, care centres, and funeral homes. The dying are tucked away and hidden from view, closed up in caskets, and obfuscated into nothingness without anyone ever having to accept the matter of death itself. 'They've gone to a better place', we might overhear; 'They're sleeping the long sleep' is another such abstraction, a phrase to distract us from the reality that is shared by all. Of course, it's of no surprise that a culture that prides itself solely on sensual pleasures would deride suffering and death to such an extent as to ignore them entirely. You can't, however, ignore reality for long. Some might consider such talk morbid, but I would argue it's only such if it's needless. There is no need to harp on about death and dying all day, especially when in the thralls of life. Yet, there is also no need to arrogantly cling to life when in the thralls of death. Everything and everyone has its time, that's just how it is and there isn't any need to be miserable about it. Yet if one *is* to assume the modern, miserable standpoint in relation to mandatory death, then it comes as no surprise that Christianity (and many other religions) with its continual references to death and suffering is off-putting.

However, death brings forth a strict limit regarding our personal potential, with suffering as its momentary reminder: We shall not be here for long and we have a certain amount of time with which to work, what shall we do? And herein is the problem with modernity's wilful ignorance of death. Death affords us a mandatory question that we can either choose to ignore or choose to integrate, *who are we to be*? We have a limited timeline and can only decide, conserve, and build so much. But when that limit is ignored and all act as if the party shall go on forever before one knows it death is there waiting and nothing has been crystallised. Ignorance of death, then, entails a sole reverence of life, a life that shall end. In time I will get to specific questions relating to the afterlife, but leaving those aside for now we need to look at our current, modern presuppositions regarding what may happen after death. For most, it seems, we are solely material beings and as such we shall simply erode back into the dirt and the whole thing will have been for nought except for a few parties here and there. Some may believe in determinate stops such as heaven and hell. Some others may believe in reincarnation or rebirth. As I'm focusing on Christianity I will, further along, be focusing on heaven and hell, but the question remains, what of death and the afterlife in the modern world? If you are reading this book then I assume you have felt that calling for the elusive 'something more' in your heart, and are at the very least open to some possibility of life after death. Put simply, death can be thought of as that moment wherein the relationship between the body and the soul is critically changed. This, in turn, leads us to that funny, archaic word 'soul'. A word that feels almost antithetical to what it is to be modern.

The soul in the modern world

We may hear of the soul, a soul, or just plain 'soul' in romantic terms within contemporary society. We may even overhear someone stating that someone else has a good soul, promoting a meaning wherein the term soul becomes synonymous with authenticity or essence. When we speak of souls within the modern materialist world we are not thinking of the breath of God or the Light of the Divine, but a psychological reference for something 'deeper'. In reality, ripped from its theological foundation, the term soul does become just that aforementioned romantic (but flimsy) signification of that 'something' we can't actually determine about someone.

Though I will spend time later defining it, from the point of view of this book the soul belongs to the spiritual world. Thus, from a purely materialist perspective, there is little use for it, especially considering it's not a material reality. This reduction of all things to the material plane of existence may seem like a simple matter of scraping away religious thinking, but the loss of the soul has equally invited the loss of conscience or at least the act of needing to listen to one's voice of conscience. This isn't to say that moderns are unable to act ethically, only that the support to which those ethical acts make sense has since been forgotten or denied. There will be those of course who would argue that my argument doesn't follow and that the modern world has got along fine without the need for the soul. I would accept this as mostly true, other than the fact that the primary ethical system by which the modern (Western) world abides is still emphatically Christian. We have not—despite Nietzsche's proclamation of the death of God—simply cast aside the 10 Commandments or the Beatitudes; Christ Himself is held up as the ultimate ethical figure, and the majority of social etiquette and ethical acts are based upon our respective Christian understanding of them. We collectively agree (with some extreme outliers) that it is good and virtuous to be kind, charitable, humble, forgiving, courageous, patient, diligent, loving, and honest, without once noticing that the very ethics that we (by default) agree are good are those our culture has derived from Christian history, or at least our understanding of *how* these acts are virtuous is an emphatically Christian understanding. It is a morality that has become tautological, we would perhaps go so far as to say there isn't a need to unearth the meaning behind kindness, we just *know* it's good to be kind. A testament to Christianity to be sure, and yet equally a testament to the ongoing process of secularisation's ability to occlude that which has transparently spiritual roots.

See, now we come to think of it, very few of those aforementioned virtues make much sense if understood in relation to the modern world's own values. It is, however, quite the task to draw out the values of the modern world, not because of its distinct lack of values but due to its inherent flexibility. The difference to be emphasised here is between values/virtues given and values/virtues revealed. The Christian values were not revealed throughout time by way of cultural or individual selection with respect to specific contexts, they were metaphorically given to—or written onto—the human heart by God; they are that which haunts us in the background in moments of decision. Whereas modern values, on the other hand, are revealed by way of socio-cultural selection (inclusive of a large amount of selection *from* Christian standards of ethics) evolution, cooperation, and contemporaneous whims (progress). However, the values of the modern world that the majority of people aspire to are, unsurprisingly, material: careerism, wealth building, property-owning, border development, pleasure-seeking, and inebriation are but some of those things the modern masses seek.

What this has to do with the soul will be made clear soon, but when written out in such contradistinction, is it not almost miraculous that Christian virtues even exist within our society today? Not a single one of them coheres with modern values, and yet, mostly, they reign triumphant. So why is it that modern values have not entirely overtaken and we are not all simply at each other's throats for the next paycheque? One argument would be that human beings are intrinsically good and that despite our material interests we succumb to the ethically good choice. From experience I can't for a minute take this to be true. As such, I put forth a second argument—it is the inherent flexibility of modern values that in turn immediately negates them. We could work at an amazing job or we could live simply; we could live alone or build a community; we could seek pleasure or become an ascetic; we could be drunk or sober; we could—as per the modern understanding of freedom as a *pure* choice—do anything we damn well please; and yet, from the viewpoint of modernity, there's no foundational reason to do this *or* that. Outside of fickle personal preference or spur-of-the-moment pleasure-seeking, there appears little reason to shoot for a specific aim over any other. Kindness, in the grand scheme of things, seems a far better use of one's time than a selection of choices that all amount to nothing. But why this failure? Why are the modern world's values so transparently impotent?

The reason is that moderns, in refusing limitation and death, unconsciously adhere to a material openness and flexibility that knows no bounds and thus has nothing to work with or against. Pure freedom is pure friction. If one hasn't accepted the boundary of death as *the* event of definition ('Who shall I become?'), then what remains is solely moment-to-moment evasion of worth. This is where we need to bring the soul back into the discussion for clarification. The soul as that metaphorical indexer of morality, piety, and love is the ever-present end for each and every Christian. I state that it's ever-present for the fact the soul—as part of the divine—is *already of* the eternity that shall arrive after death; one's soul is *already* well on its way to heaven or hell *via* our actions now—you're *already* in eternity, you're just waiting for your body to degrade! As such, Christians carry death with them throughout life by way of understanding that their body is merely a material vessel for use by the soul. The soul cannot act of its own accord and so we have the limited time of the body to bolster its piety (so to speak). And so, the soul, acting as an ever-present internal end begets, in moments of decision, a reminder of finality and therein of deeper, God-written worth in relation to values. If you remove the soul (by way of declaring material king), you remove man's purpose and therein deflate all values to nil.

And so here I find myself quite saddened by the paradox of modern man, at least in terms of his ethical decision-making. There are, of course, those who are faced with a decision that has drowned out the noise of the conscience so thoroughly that modern values abide and greed, hate, and cruelty reign supreme. But such people seem to be in the minority. It appears—once again from experience (yours may differ)—that when faced with this decision between Christian and modern values, many would still opt for kindness or humility, despite the fact that from their default worldview, such a decision makes no sense. This is the paradox modern man finds himself in, making seemingly nonsensical decisions without any recourse as to why. The decisions can therein only make sense once the soul—as a serious theological teleological motor (once again, a metaphor)—has been reinstated as sincere. It isn't all bad of course, the Good is always the Good whatever form it takes, it would simply be far more productive if it could once again find its rightful home, away from systems that seek to brutalise it as a means to beget more worldly values.

The Christian virtues are of the Divine and of the soul. Severed from this origin and left floating within modernity they become nonsensical, signals ready to be abused and used for the sake of more elusive modern values such as status or popularity. God is infinite and eternal; He is not *in* time at certain junctures but is beyond time. As such, to sever such virtues from their Creator is to contextualise them to history and transform them into a fetish. *Grasping* at the Good we rip it from its root like a flower from its stem, and it becomes simultaneously ours and rotten; we have drawn it into time and it is already decaying. Such is the case with *all forms* of Christian politicisation. You slice the Word from the page and Goodness from the heavens and draw them both down to the world as to become word and *tradition*. The political impetus to 'return' is just this, a case of seeking specific, historical, temporal, and therefore worldly goodness long-since severed and fit only for a certain time and place, and therein desiring to drag it forward to an unfit time as to capture, control, and disprove. Yet no one ever stops to ask why there is such a *traditional* need to artificially fold history like this as a means to impose ethics when the greatest God-given tool for such decisions is found within all human beings and was placed there by God Himself, the heart, the soul. Do you distrust your own conscience to such a degree that you prefer word to usurp Word, or is it possible that long-lost words out of context allow you to drown out that Voice within and promote your personally preferred worldly aims?

The Reformation, the sacred, and Couliano

For me there are a few glaring questions lingering behind the discussion thus far: How was it that the sacred came to fall away and allow the profane to take over our collective understanding of the world? What happened to the sacred potency of terms such as soul and prayer? Where has the sacred gone? To name but a few. There is, undoubtedly, extensive literature on this topic, often focusing primarily on the transition from a predominantly religious society to a predominantly secular one. But this isn't the angle I wish to home in on. I want to address the specific degradation of what might be titled the sacred or 'earthy' elements of Christianity. The decline of the spiritual potential and feeling within man in favour of quantification and material certainty. For theorisation to open up this strange flip of religious ideals I shall turn to a somewhat infamous text by Ioan P. Couliano, his 1987 book *Eros and Magic in the Renaissance* (1988).

At the beginning of Chapter 9 of that book, in a section titled 'Abolition of the phantasmic', Couliano coheres to various threads that have arisen throughout the book thus far and solidifies them into one of the book's major theses. Via liberal reform, Luther came to reduce imagery and 'external forms of ritual in order to concentrate on inward religious experience' (1988, p. 192). With (for Couliano) 'the most important goal of ... root[ing] out the cult of idols from the [Catholic] Church' (1988, p. 193). For Couliano this leads to a complete censorship of the imaginary and of phantasms, those things which Couliano posits as transforming the five senses into messages perceptible to the soul. As such, without these phantasms, the soul can understand nothing of the world. Nothing of the external can be brought to be understood by the internal. In short, the great tyranny of the Reformation for Couliano was not primarily political or ecclesiastical, but truly spiritual, if not *internal*. It was a usurping of that *inner sense* that connects us in an 'earthy', soulful way to the Divine.

However, Couliano's reading does not stop here. He asks us, what was the reaction of the Catholic Church and its Counter-Reformation? Was it to hold fast and defend ritual? Not at all, it merely replicates the quantified and material impetus of the Reformation on its own ground, leading both 'sides' of Christianity at that juncture heading forward without any difference where spiritual depth is concerned.

I haven't the ground to go too deep into the intricacies of Couliano's text here, but I place this quick thesis here as a historic marker of change. Wherein—once again, for Couliano—institutional Christianity becomes its own tyrant, mimetically infecting itself with the contemporaneous attitudes of the day, whilst simultaneously shedding itself of anything it feels may hamper its progression into the future. At this point in time, I would argue, Christianity comes head-to-head with the modern world and instead of believing its rituals as Truth in themselves, institutionally seeks to quickly occlude them in the hopes of continuing its status and popularity amidst cultural change. One could possibly argue that it was this transition that allowed institutional Christianity 100–200 years later to manage a coexistence with the Industrial Revolution that may have otherwise been impossible. Yet such a possibility of coexistence—that is, if you agree with Couliano's thesis—merges the sacred and the profane, makes a mockery of the spirit-material duality, leaving us, where exactly?

If it is that the sacred and the profane have come to *co*exist, therein denying the inherent hierarchy afforded the spiritual/divine ever since man has written of God, then we are left with but a single, homogenised world from which to draw our conclusions. From such a world it comes as no surprise that materialism wins the day and becomes the default worldview, for the fact that in *merging* the sacred with the profane, the former is drawn *down* to the level of material, and thus symbol becomes a sign, ritual becomes play, and prayer becomes psyche. Now this isn't to say that by entering into that long-since lost inner life one need cast aside all that is material, only that in allowing oneself to be brought *up* to God is equally to realise the folly of the world in all its impermanence.

It is this merged world we currently live in. Little has changed since the historical events of the Reformation, Counter-Reformation, and Industrial Revolution other than the acceleration of the material ideals it presupposed. Yet, as we all will have heard, *'The Kingdom of God is within you'* (Luke 17:21), and so there is no need to uproot civilisations to find God when He is there all along. It is this reconnection I hope to make possible. The sacred, then, utilising Couliano's thesis as my foundation, was subsumed into the infighting of the Reformation and exists today somewhat battered and hidden. However, it is not so much a case of attempting to find it behind certain dogma, but a matter of having the strength and purity to *reveal* it from behind all the materialist nonsense long-since drilled into our average modern minds. It is a case of paying attention to how modern life abuses its authority and negates a multiplicity of feelings and sensations we apparently have no internal language. And if it is such that one cannot articulate their internal—sacred—feelings within the bounds of empirical chatter then supposedly the world just agrees they must not exist altogether. Don't fall for such folly! Trust your own heart, your own voice, and your own relationship with God and the Divine.

Alternative spiritual currents

Before heading forwards there is one more factor I feel I should tackle, that of other religions and spiritual currents. As has already been made clear, my own journey towards and—in a sense—through Christian institutions has led me to a highly open understanding of Christianity. One that now seeks to approach all things from the position of love, spiritual growth, and subjective context as opposed to dogma. Of course, those who are theologically minded and find their faith strictly within dogma will be quick to corral my efforts here as merely incorrect as opposed to a different perspective. Dogmatism is inherently self-limiting. It is a prison that begets its own walls. As comforting as it may be whilst one's own natural inclinations are in abidance to the intricacies of dogma, the day will arrive when one can no longer manage to remove or crush that part of them that doesn't fit. At that juncture it will *seem* as if one has—if they wish to remain in their *exact* dogmatic position—a choice of either repression or exit. When one doesn't fit as they understand they should, one is likely to muster all the energy they can to shove down or away that thing in them that doesn't quite work or throw the baby out with the bathwater and call quits on the whole endeavour. There is, however, the third option that I subtly mentioned earlier—take a step back, assess the larger picture, remember where you started and why you set foot on the mountain in the first place and take a breather, then assess whether or not an alteration to the route may work.

One may be wondering what this has to do with other religions and spiritualities. Let me explain. I am sympathetic to the perennialist worldview, a philosophical and spiritual viewpoint that sees all religious traditions as deriving their knowledge and teaching from a common, metaphysical reality or genesis. In short, the Truth is the Truth, the Good is the Good, etc. So one part of my inability to completely fit into the dogma of many religious institutions is that I would be equally accepting of another's religious path. Who am I to say that the lifelong Muslim, Sikh, or Buddhist is wrong? Would they not simply flip the exact same logic onto me, wherein both proclaim the other *incorrect* and move on with our lives? What does this have to do with God, spirit, Truth, or love—nothing! My disdain for dogma is related to the distinction between correctness and understanding. Those who bellow out tradition and countless theological texts one has never heard of often do so for the sake of being *right* as opposed to actually entering a conversation of understanding. 'I'm right, you're wrong!' is the perspective of an insolent child, not someone who is spiritually growing. In the words of St Edith Stein, 'Do not accept anything as the truth if it lacks love. And, do not accept anything as love which lacks truth'.

Herein is one of the gravest errors modern Christianity has made, especially regarding its parishioners and newcomers. The common public conflation of the *entirety* of Christianity with a single facet of its teaching, namely, its moral teaching. When people think of Christianity they think of rules, laws, and commandments. They think of *Thou shalt not!* And there is so much more, there is the community, the Sacraments, liturgy, hymns, prayer, the symbolism, the potential for growth and purpose, and the joy. Yet, for many, the Church is little more than a textbook of morals ready to damn us into oblivion. And so is it any wonder that so many do not even approach the spirit—let alone a Church—not from any worldly anxiety, but from their inability to live up to the standards of God who *is* Himself those very standards?

For me, this fear is critically misplaced, and here I will explain why I've placed this digression in this section on other religions. Once again, for me, a relationship with God or the Divine is just that, a relationship. It's there to make me a better person, help me grow, and allow me to understand the world with greater depth. The love in this relationship is reciprocal. I love (or, put energy towards) God, He loves me. But imagine if such a relationship transforms in such a way that I feel I am only doing so out of obligation, worldly fear, or guilt. There can be nothing that can be definitely called 'love' to arise from any of these states, and yet this is where many find themselves and this is why so many throw in the towel. They feel they cannot live up to God's standard because God *is* morality itself and so any betrayal of ethics or etiquette is a betrayal of quite literally ... everything. The slightest digression from institutionally imposed rules becomes a cause for a serious crisis. Is this love? I would not say so. We need to return to the spirit, to the basic love and teaching of Jesus Christ. For in beginning with dogma, morals, and specific churches, we are assuming the spiritual foundation that leads to those things yet does *not* arise from them.

So what of other religions and currents? Maybe there is another book of this sort for those new to other faiths who would equally consider Christianity another Truth to be found. What works for one may not work for another and no man can be arm-wrestled to God. One cannot deny their heart and there will come a time for all when dogma comes up against love. There *are* other religions. Other people practice them and that works for them. Some people of one religion will argue all should believe in their God, some of another religion will say the same of their God, and many Christians would call me a heretic for being open in this manner. So what is one to do? Simply what they can.

There are tasks and duties for the children of God that are difficult enough without yet more schism getting in the way. It appears it's much easier to write and lecture on why one's tradition is so great and right than to check in on the lonely old lady next door. The grand narratives of dense theology rarely raise their heads amidst daily life, and yet they are often all we hear about and repeatedly used as a means to stamp out conversation. It is far easier to be abstractly correct than practically loving.

I'm not here to argue for this-or-that denomination, this-or-that church. Christ is a figure of love and hope who is always needed and I'm here to bring Him before other's eyes once more. Do I think I can prove the existence of God or make someone believe? No. I'm here to give you a glimpse down the path and let you decide for yourself—via some very simple exercises—whether or not it might be worth exploring.

What Christianity isn't

Before we get to the spiritual stuff, however, there is but another digression, another case of digging out the weeds. Give thanks to public schooling for this, but before talking about Christianity in itself I need to spend a little time clarifying what it *isn't*. See, the modern world has undoubtedly made the task of writing about Christianity exceedingly difficult. Not only because the relativist foundation of the world at large is completely anathema to the teachings of Christ and various Church doctrines, but also because modernity promotes a false vacuum where education is concerned.

For instance, when we hear about people placing their children in Christian schools, or public schools teaching certain religious doctrines, we're quick to hear the retort that such practices shouldn't take place at a young age because children should be able to 'Make the choice for themselves'. In turn, we are left with the idea that modern education is somehow a complete vacuum, a blank slate from which the pupil in question develops their own personal beliefs and ideas. The reality, of course, is far different. Schooling, as with any other institution, has its own agenda and veils its own dogma under the guise of terms such as socialisation. Avoiding the idea that it's anything but a new form of secular religion, complete with its own virtues of pride, blind obedience, learned helplessness, and selfishness.

The purpose of this short tirade on modern education isn't placed here for its own sake, for if we're to get to the heart of what Christianity *is*, and what it means therefore to *be* a Christian, then I must first uproot many of the misconceptions concerning Christianity which schooling—very subtly—programmed into us. In short, we cannot begin our journey to Christ if we are to (ironically) pre-judge Him in our approach.

Christianity isn't exactly popular anymore, and though I don't agree with the oft-pushed idea that Christians are victims, I do, however, believe that Christianity has been secularised to such an extent as to become just one of many other various pastimes which people might choose to undertake. Modern education—as with many ideas which don't fit its mould—doesn't teach Christianity with respect to its own teachings (those of Jesus Christ), but haphazardly filters the doctrine of the Church through its own presumptions, leading many potential Christians (myself included) into a state of, at first, confusion, then second, apathy, and finally, rejection. If one attempts to teach and understand Christianity from the materialist, empiricist, and textually literalist framework of the modern world, they are simply going to end up head-to-head with a mass of contradictions.

This materialist understanding of Christianity has led to many of the common appreciations of Christianity such as God being an 'old man in the sky', that Christianity is anti-science, or that the Bible magically came down from heaven. I'm hoping that throughout this book, by unspooling these misconceptions about Christianity by way of warmly teaching its most basic principles you may come to realise that your understanding of Christianity isn't necessarily incorrect, as much as it's literally just *not* what Christianity is at all. Many of these misconceptions are largely related to the social role of the Christian within the world, but the first, that God is a 'big man in the sky', is a theological matter and of the utmost importance, and so there I shall begin as to lay a small foundation going forward of how a single misconception regarding 'God' can drastically occlude the truth of faith.

On the term 'God'

Yet, before going forward with this critique of God as understood as an 'old man in the sky'—and this book in general—I want to make it clear that I am equally critical of the word 'God'. It is perhaps the trickiest signifier in existence for the fact it is attempting to represent the unrepresentable; it is attempting to give finite relation to He or That which begets the infinite possibility of relation itself. In short, the term God seeks to define the undefinable. The problem with signifiers and words is that they themselves are inherently material, they fly out from our fleshy mouths into others' ears, they fall from our fingertips onto the corporeal page, and, at that juncture, become nothing more than language. The problem with language is quite simple: The description of a cup of coffee is *not* the same as the experience of a cup of coffee. Words will always fall short and it is not until any singular individual tastes the cup of coffee for themselves that they begin to actually *experience* it and therefore understand it. The same is true of God. In fact, one might say God is the original case of this language-experience paradox. Many may argue that it has just become a commonly agreed-upon word so that we all know what we're referring to, despite the fact that (far and away from the simplicity of a humble cup of coffee) one's own experience of God may differ drastically from someone else's. Often to such a degree that the question of definition is best left alone.

In fact, the further I entered into my own relationship with God and attempted discussion of it with other people, I found that terms such as Unity, Harmony, Absolute, the Most-High, or the Most-Holy became more agreeable to me. Not because such names alter or constrain the definition towards a specific understanding, but on the contrary they allow the overarching term God to expand its meaning in multiple directions, often away from a notably anthropocentric definition towards one which encompassed all and everything.

I would go so far as to say that if someone were to ask me Who or What it is I pray to, I would reply simply with silence. This isn't me being coy or deliberately mysterious, but simply that the *experience* of prayer (especially 'open prayer' which I will get to) is one's own, and any attempt to say 'I am praying to *this* exact thing' is immediately thwarted with error for the fact it (the sentence and signifier) *isn't* the experience. In a way, it's this definitive attitude towards God that I hope to somewhat question throughout this book. Many would state that this is merely an anti-dogmatic position and that I wish to avoid the uncomfortable aspects of tradition. But before any such worship, reading, and adherence to dogmatics is underway, all that one has is oneself and one's experience. And try as hard as one might to pretend that their self is in alignment with a dogma far off or as of yet misunderstood, the resulting incompatibility will always be a failure. I speak about this phenomenon much later on, calling it the 'Saintly Ideal'.

But, before going forward, if you approach the undefinable, unmanifested, and infinite 'God' with definitions, worldly manifestations, and a finite constriction in relation to your openness to Him, all you're going to meet is paradox and anxiety. Maybe it is the case that after all one's reading of dogmatics, ye olde catechisms, and traditional texts that the God one finds in prayer fits this education one-to-one, and all the words put to paper happen to match the Word. But this may also *not* happen, in which case one is left only with a mass of contradictions which they then have to try to fit God into, an undertaking that is by definition impossible. The key here is to never conflate the sign with that which it signifies, never to stare at the symbol itself instead of prying out its meaning, and, most importantly, never to conflate word with the Word itself. The free-floating nature of the definition of God, especially in terms of one's own experiential reality, is something to hold in mind at all times whenever the term appears throughout the text. God has a unique relationship to every single soul, to every single person, and when we see the term God we should try to think about what His presence means for ourselves within the context at hand.

God is an old man in the sky

With this said, I'd like to unspool one of the most emphatically incorrect, constrained definitions ever applied to the name 'God', the idea of God being an old man in the sky. An idea that is so transparently materialistic and human-centred that it's of no surprise that it's risen to such popularity. When presented with the Christian worldview many modern people are quick to become confused because such a lifestyle makes no sense from their point of view—blind obedience to something we (apparently) can't see or sense, denial of many (seemingly) pleasurable and fun vices, and getting up early on a Sunday (amongst many other undertakings)—all seem to be nonsensical. Unable to view the world from any other perspective but their own, modern man has been quick to filter God through lenses he feels comfortable with: God becomes a 'psychological need for a father', a coping mechanism for loss, or a man in the sky. Each of these common readings of Christianity is quick to anthropomorphise God, quick to subsume Him to *our* level so that we once again have a full understanding of everything at hand,

and there's no need to panic for lack of control. Quite poignantly, worship of God—or gods, if you are so inclined—is, from the point of view of the modern world, to do with anything and everything *except* man having a connection with the Divine. Very few are introspective enough to realise that these false readings of God and Christianity are far too flimsy to ever retain their rigour at the level of faith and belief found around the world. In a constant state of panic, the modern world will happily accept *any* other theorisation of religion, faith, and belief, *other* than the fact that it may just very well be that there is a God and that billions of people speak to Him every day. Quite ironically, the 'man in the sky' argument seeks to change God in such a way that he becomes material and then concludes that because we can't see Him (materially) He therefore isn't real.

So one might now ask, 'Well, if God *is* real, but He *isn't* a man in the sky, then what is He? And still, why can't we see Him?' First, one would still be beginning their journey from the emphatically materialist worldview, subsuming everything in life to the level of cold-hard (object-level) facts, in spite of the fact countless daily occurrences are entirely devoid of what is considered to be evidence. We cannot see thoughts, intuition, heat, cold, air, hunger, feelings, pangs of conscience, intuition, dreams, atmospheres, presences, wisdom, kindness, gravity, magnetism, sound, smell, taste, and a whole host of other peculiar happenings, and yet, somehow, we *can* see and know them, but it's a form of sight and sense which we choose to simply ignore.

God isn't material, He isn't matter. God is spirit. He isn't hidden in the usual way; He just doesn't *appear* in the presumed accessible way we're used to. The answer to the question 'Well then, why doesn't He just reveal himself?' is one of *faith*, something I will delve into far more in Part 2. For now, however, one should ask themselves the question—with a clear heart and mind—*if* there is a God, and He *wants* me to know Him and Love Him (which He does), and also *He* wants to take a step towards me, why doesn't He just do that? The answer is, once again, faith. If one doesn't have faith in God, believe that He is there for them, love Him, and desire to know Him of their own volition, their own search for Truth, then in what sense would one even be able to recognise God if He was right there in front of them? If one doesn't wish to see, they simply won't be able to. Alongside this is the usual follow-up retort, 'Well, God could just *make* me love Him!' Now, technically, yes, He could. However, this would negate the entire teaching and Love of God. The Lord gave us free will, He gave us individuality, and the ability to make our own personal choices and so to *make* us love Him would be the equivalent of stating you love him with a gun to your head, and hopefully we would all understand that such proclamations of love which are forced can never be sincere. Christianity, then, isn't merely a weekly lecture on everything you've done wrong. Nor is it the equivalent of a mediation service for some abstract watchman in the sky. It is a faith and *then* a religion based upon the Life of Jesus Christ.

I will expand more upon what Christianity *is* very soon, but as one can see, the answers I've given here tend to go around in circles. If either side is leaning too far their way (atheists into materialism or Christians into faith), the tendency is for both to look past one another and make no headway in actual understanding. I will be so bold as to offer a bridge at this juncture between atheism and Christianity, between nothingness and God, between material and Christ. The bridge is simple, sincere, and quiet, its name is prayer. If you are an atheist or an agnostic reading this, perhaps you feel this is a bit rich, and that I haven't done enough to appease your worldview. As I stated in the beginning, I was a militant atheist for many years and I know full well that once that perspective is locked in there is practically nothing to be done and you just continue on in your atheistic state, despite often feeling that call towards something *more*. And so if you feel it wrong for me to offer prayer as an answer here without offering an atheist equivalent then may I be so bold as to ask the believers reading this to ... not believe in God for a minute or two? Those who are reading this and have faith they will understand how absurd such a 'practice' is, that's simply not how faith works. But that I will get to. For now, let me discuss this bridge a little more and give you something to do before reading on.

The bridge here is a practice and that practice is prayer. To begin crossing this bridge the task at hand is a simple one. *Say a single prayer.* Perhaps you've never said a prayer before in your life and the entire idea of doing so feels alien to you, humiliating, ridiculous, silly, absurd, maybe it even goes against everything you've ever built up within yourself. But you picked up this book for a reason and despite quite liking what I've written throughout this text, nothing here adds up to a *single* sincere prayer. All you need do is this:

* * *

Exercise 1

Go off and find a quiet place where you can go and *be* on your own. It doesn't need to be a mountain retreat or a chapel, it can just be your sofa or even your car; in fact, you could even say this prayer walking in quiet woods. Sit down, kneel, or walk quietly, settle yourself internally by trying to quieten those annoying demands of the world which are whizzing around your brain, and say to them 'I will deal with you later, just give me a couple of minutes right now', and you might find they give you some patience. And now, before your actual prayer, try to bring to the fore the reason why you might have *already* reached out to God by reading my book. Why do you find yourself really hoping at this moment? Try to bring to the fore the absurdity, confusion, and lack of *that something more* you consistently find within the modern world and your current life. Focus on how that *feels*. And now, at this point ... say your prayer. If you are textually minded and want to state a more official prayer then there is none better than the *Our Father*, also known as the *Lord's Prayer*:

> *Our Father who art in heaven,*
> *hallowed be thy name.*
> *Thy kingdom come,*
> *Thy will be done*
> *on earth, as it is in heaven.*
> *Give us this day our daily bread,*
> *and forgive us our trespasses,*
> *as we forgive those who trespass against us,*
> *and lead us not into temptation,*
> *but deliver us from evil.*
> *Amen.*

You may wish to speak directly to God in a conversation, tell Him your worries and concerns, and what you may be hoping for regarding the future. Another very spiritually productive possibility is praying to God *for* faith, asking God to know Him better. Many don't realise this and assume that faith and belief just 'are', and that if one is without them well ... that's it for them! Absolutely not true. One can always ask God for faith and help in all spiritual matters. Or, finally, one could just sit and *open oneself* to God by way of simply saying 'I Am Here' and seeing what comes (this would be my preference). It's up to you. Doesn't need to be long. Just a single prayer. After you have said your prayer, simply go about your day.

* * *

See, I could reel off a multitude of various complex proofs for the existence of God which are left out from nearly all school curriculums. There are the Thomist, Augustinian, Neo-Platonic, Leibnitzian (Rationalist), and Aristotelian proofs. There is the argument from design, the first cause argument, the cosmological argument, the ontological argument, the argument from beauty, the argument from induction, and … you get the picture. One could read theological, philosophical, and logical arguments for the existence of God all day and they would only give one an unbalanced form of false certainty that is only intellectual. For many people, these theoretical arguments suffice in terms of personal faith and I must emphasise that such forms of argumentation *are* needed, one shouldn't enter into faith solely off the basis of an indescribable presence—for how would you know what it was? However, in a world where information regarding all the aforementioned arguments is at our fingertips, I believe that what is stopping people from *believing* in God isn't a lack of knowledge, but a lack of relation. Sure, we have book after book on theology, but one may still ask how it is they can come to actually know Him, in themselves. And the answer to *that* question is not intellectual, but experiential. An experience that is found within a single prayer.

What Christianity is

Moving forward from these abstract misunderstandings of Christianity, the reader may find themselves asking the very same questions I myself asked as I set foot on my spiritual journey—'Well, what's this all about then?' Christian ideas, morals, and stories are so deeply embedded within our culture, along with thousands of years of subjective interpretation, that it's often difficult—as with most things—to get to the heart of the matter. So in this section, I seek to give you the reader some overviews of the basics of Christianity without any fluff attached, so that before proceeding into the strictly spiritual sections in Part 2, one will have a stable Christian language to take with them.

In a sense the answer to the 'what' of Christianity is surprisingly simple, the answer is Christ. The social place of religion is important, the history of the Church is both positively and negatively illuminating, the lives of the Saints and the Apostles are all blueprints for leading lives of purity and goodness, and yet, the truth of the matter is that all such histories, ideas, and books have been formed around a single figure, the person known as Jesus Christ. I feel it important to understand Christ as a figure for the fact I cannot state He was solely a man, for He was both man and God incarnate. In short, Christianity, in all its beauty, mystery, and wonder began under the most delicate of circumstances; a religion that currently has 2.38 billion members—roughly one-third of the world's population—began from the teachings of a single individual. Spreading to 12 extremely faithful, yet oh-so-human Apostles, and slowly spreading throughout the globe.

It is difficult for us moderns to look at Christianity with anything but tainted eyes. For us, Christianity has become little more than another in a long past (and long future) of various seemingly vague spiritual practices, which seek only to appease or brush away the problems of the human heart. The way we currently look at the world leaves no room for mystery or the sacred. Everything is mediated into our materialist minds and hastily deconstructed so as to remain palpable; we are quick to consume and retain control. Amidst modernity, God, creation, spirits, angels, prayer, and the afterlife are understood at best as unconscious myths, and at worst socio-cultural relics of some more archaic time. Even the most minute jot of mystery is fed into the thresher of science, knowledge, and quantification, sliced-and-diced, and retrieved at the other side entirely unrecognisable, and yet supposedly absolutely disproved. Despite our oft-declared virtues of tolerance, openness, and intrigue, the only reason we moderns *cannot* accept regarding the existence of religion, faith, and God, is that it may just very well be that God exists. The modern mind can only approach God if *it* is in control, and in such a case, God disappears. But this I shall get to.

But why does this continual focus on God and the modern world? Why, in talking about Christianity *is* do I feel this to be of such importance? First, 'times change', as the saying goes. Thus, to appreciate Christianity via books of old is helpful in a historically progressive sense (How did we get here?), but it isn't necessarily helpful in a practical sense. It's all well and good to read about the Saints, bishops, and communities of old with admiration, but it's been quite some time since such a Christian culture has been truly embedded within society. In quite the same way that one can only begin with themselves, so too can one only begin with the society at hand, the one they live in. Anything else is a matter of attending to reality with an ideal long-since lost. There are many practical, daily examples I could use here regarding the relationship between Christianity and the modern world: prayer, charity, Mass, Confession, or making the sign of the Cross, but I shall use the Bible. Not in any scriptural sense, nor as a trajectory to understand

Christianity in itself, but first as a means to unpick our internal knot of secularity.

If one is to travel practically anywhere in the world where there is civilisation, anywhere there is a hotel, or anywhere there is access to books, the chances are *extremely* high that one will be in close proximity to the object we collectively call 'the Bible'. Due to the modern world's ignorance of the sacred and holy, this thing we call 'the Bible' has become, in our collective thought, little more than some odd relic of the past, an object so common we rarely spare it a thought—unless of course we have faith. For sincere Christians however, this thing we all know about and are aware of called 'the Bible' is *literally* a Holy Book. Its two books called the Old Testament and the New Testament are quite literally products of divine inspiration. This book, the Bible, which has by estimation been distributed 5 billion times, has become so commonplace, it has been so profaned, that each and every one of us is each day within mere metres of the Word of God, and yet we pass on by as if it were nothing but another object.

There are many other books declared holy by other religions, some with large followings, others with small ones. We in the West have perhaps the same familiarity with the Quran, the Holy Book of Islam, and would equally walk on by. Perhaps, due to personal contexts, there are other such Holy Books we've become so accustomed to that they exist as just another object in the world. But what if, as a strange theoretical experiment, we were to try to revert our understanding of the Bible? To alter the way we perceive with respect to its holy contents? The Bible found in a hotel drawer, or slumped in a supermarket donations book pile is a strange phenomenon indeed when one thinks about it. If we were to replace the Bible in such instances—this oh-so-common 'book'—with other more supposedly mysterious, peculiar, and esoteric holy texts we might find ourselves asking what in the world we are reading. If we were to enter our hotel room for the weekend to find a copy of *The Book of the Law* on our bedside table, or *The Hermetica* in the bottom of the wardrobe, or the *Principia Discordia* tucked under the bed, we might ask ourselves what it is we've found. We would open such texts with a strange feeling of foreignness and possibly even adventure. We would enter these worlds with a mind clear of presumptions for the fact we haven't been born into a culture which delimits our understanding. The Bible (and Christianity), as many of us well know, and some of us may be thinking, is a different case altogether. *We know* what these things are we tell ourselves. We've no need to venture down such a path because we already understand. What if we were to step back?

You awake one morning and suddenly the world has changed so that you have never heard of Christianity, haven't a clue what the Bible is, and have no memory of anything adjacent to these things. You're off on a very important business trip and have planned to stay in a hotel overnight. You arrive at the hotel, check in, and grab a quick bite to eat, all before heading to your room to retire for the night. Plonking yourself on the bed you don't feel all that tired yet, but for some reason the TV isn't working. In bored desperation you begin looking aimlessly around the room, happening to slide open the top drawer of your bedside table. In it, you find a leather-bound book. Embossed in gold on the front cover are the words HOLY BIBLE. When you come to think about it, you're not entirely sure what these words mean. You sit back on the bed, open it up at the first page, and are swiftly whisked away into an admittedly strange, beautiful, and often terrifying tale regarding the creation and life of everything existing.

You follow the creation of your world, through various prophetic narratives, and things called miracles before you reach *The Book of the New Testament*. Here you learn of a God-man called Jesus Christ who was the literal Son of God, part of something called the Trinity, and died from crucifixion for our sins. You learn of life after death, the Apostles, the purpose of life, and what is to be done, and find various answers to the deep discontentment you rarely admit haunts you. Maybe you are quick to reach for your phone, in disbelief that such things can be. Quick to Google the evidence for God and Scripture, hasty to try to understand how miracles can be.

I would argue that if such an event *could* happen; if such an untarnished mind approached the Bible in this way, such a person wouldn't be able to move until they finished the text. And yet, we live in a world wherein 5 billion copies of this very same book exist, and we walk past them as if they are little more than a mystery novel. Of course, even in our approach to this imaginative scenario we are bringing our already formed modern minds with us, skewing it to our preferences, and attempting to control it.

* * *

Exercise 2

In this exercise we are simply going to try to look at what it is *we* are bringing to Christianity (or even God/spirituality in general). Spend 15–30 minutes thinking about what your religious education—both inside and outside of school—has been like. Once again, find somewhere quiet and ask yourself the following questions, see what other questions arise. Maybe there will be answers, maybe there won't. It may help to write down your thoughts.

What is my attitude regarding God?

What are the attitudes regarding God you see around you?

What does my family think of God?

Do friends and family believe in an afterlife?

In what way might earlier experiences negate God as a possibility?

Why is it that I may have never spent much time thinking about such topics?

What would God mean to me?

How would God being involved in the world change things?

What does it mean to be 'spiritual'?

Why have you not asked yourself these questions before?

Journal your findings.

* * *

The Old and New Testaments

Hopefully, with a little more dust cleared away, let's begin to look at the content of Christianity. As I suggested earlier, the Bible is a Holy Book that has become profane. Seen and spoken about so commonly and lazily that it becomes just another thing for us to reference. But the Bible is not just some-or-other text filled with inspirational ideas and stories; it is *divinely inspired*. There's a lot to unpack here, and I mostly seek to do so as a means, once again, to dispel many of the misunderstandings of Christianity. Because one of the common, oddly enchanted ideas regarding the Bible is that it is a book Christians believe to have somehow descended from heaven, a magical text without a human author. In fact, many atheists often criticise the Bible because of the obvious 'human fingerprint' of its content.

This criticism doesn't hold water because there *is* a human fingerprint within the Bible, precisely because it was written by humans. The difference being, however, that it was written by humans who were *divinely inspired*. Even though the words of the Bible were practically written by men, the Inspiration to write the content was directly afforded them as a grace from God, and thus the words are the Word of God, or—arguably—as close to the Word as is materially possible in text. And so, even though it was written down by men, the true author is God.

As such, when one reads the Bible, they are quite literally reading Scripture handed to us by the Lord as a gift. The Bible in its complete form is understood as what God wanted/wants to communicate to us in our own language.

So that's *why* the content is so important, why it is holy, but what of the actual content? What are all these Testaments, Gospels, and books we keep hearing about? The easiest way to understand all these books is in relation to *the* event of all time, the coming of our Lord Jesus Christ. Simply put, everything is divided between the before and after of God's incarnation as Jesus Christ on earth. The Bible, then, is made up of 72 books, 45 of which were written prior to Christ's time on earth. These are the books of the Old Testament. The other 27, were, of course, written after Christ lived on earth, recording all which was given from the mouth of Christ himself and from the teachings of his Apostles. These books are collected in what we call the New Testament. Okay, fairly simple. But what *is* a Testament? For these aren't simply textual collections of historical documents, these are Testaments in the sense that they are *covenants*, or agreements with the Lord from man. The history from the Old Testament (which prophesied the coming of Christ) through to the New Testament is the covenant and promise God has made to man, and likewise that man can make to God if he so chooses. Within the New Testament is found what is called 'the Gospels', these are episodic, first-hand narratives regarding the teachings and actions of Jesus Christ, and are likely most people's entry point into the Bible. These are of such great importance because unlike the other parts of the Bible which are equally divinely inspired, the Gospels relate to Jesus Christ (God) first-hand and thus reveal to us the literal teachings of God from His own lips, from when He walked the earth.

Okay, so we understand *why* it's important, and loosely how that importance relates to the history of man, but what do we *do* with it? Here we might do well to try to take a step back and understand that it is not what *we* can do with the Bible, but what we allow *It* to do to us. In this manner, the Bible is less a Holy Book to be *used* by way of being perceived as a tool to skew the world to one's vision, but a divine blueprint regarding what it is to be moral and good altogether. So let us turn to the Bible for instruction. Before we find our home, before we set off, we need guidance, and for Christians that comes from God, and within the Bible we find the teachings the Lord Himself—as incarnated as Jesus Christ—spoke to us within our world.

The Life of Christ

As I've made clear, I believe that the Bible as an object, as a 'figure of speech', has become profaned; we speak of it with such nonchalance that we forget what it is (a *Holy* Book). As an exercise to open up the depth of Scripture, I've taken here multiple passages from the New Testament as a means to delve into the Life of Jesus Christ whilst also anchoring it within our own lives, allowing it to speak to us at our most basic, human level. Put simply, what can the Life of Christ—via Scripture—teach us about how we are to *be* Christians? Let us begin with the birth of Christ and the events leading up to it, allow me to take four lines from the Gospel of Matthew to begin to show the depth of Scripture:

> [20] *But while he thought on these things, behold the angel of the Lord appeared to him in his sleep, saying: Joseph, son of David, fear not to take unto thee Mary thy wife, for that which is conceived in her, is of the Holy Ghost.*
>
> [21] *And she shall bring forth a son: and thou shalt call his name JESUS. For he shall save his people from their sins.*
>
> [22] *Now all this was done that it might be fulfilled which the Lord spoke by the prophet, saying:*

38   A CALL TO GOD

> ²³ *Behold a virgin shall be with child, and bring forth a son, and they shall call his name Emmanuel, which being interpreted is, God with us.*
> ²⁴ *And Joseph rising up from sleep, did as the angel of the Lord had commanded him, and took unto him his wife.*
>
> (Matthew 1:20–24)

It is announced, then, that the Virgin Mary is to become pregnant, the child being Jesus. Joseph, being the man that Joseph is deals with this matter privately. This is a matter of history and Scripture, one in which Joseph's role is (understandably) sidelined with regard to the arrival of Jesus (meaning *'God with us'*). And yet, Joseph's role, and thus the beginning of the New Testament, (after the genealogy of Christ), is a signal and symbol as to the purpose and position of *man*.

We are told that *'the angel of the Lord appeared to him in his sleep'*, something which is relatively easy to understand literally, and yet a literal reading denies it its allegorical depth. For it needn't matter whether an angel appears during sleep or waking, for an angel's powers are far beyond such constraints as 'dreams'. Joseph (a man) could have been given this message via an angel at any point, anywhere, and so it can easily be argued that this aforementioned 'sleep' is symbolic. Joseph, thus—as many still are—was asleep, and to be asleep is to exist within a world of fantasy, illusion, seemingly-real hallucinations, and dreams. It perhaps need not matter whether Joseph was actually sleeping (in bed), or sleep-walking/daydreaming (still asleep) in an awakened state, for he was still, symbolically, asleep. This is to say, he was existing in a state of fantasy, not fully aware or conscious of reality.

The angel appears and tells him the news of the coming of Christ, *'And Joseph rising up from sleep, did as the angel of the Lord had commanded him, and took unto him his wife'*. It's quite strange to read this. Joseph doesn't 'wake up', which would denote a normal form of sleeping, but he 'rises up' from sleep. In an act of obedience to something higher than him, Joseph is drawn (or perhaps draws himself—or perhaps a synthesis of both) *above* sleep, he is no longer in the lower reality of imagination and fantasy but is drawn upwards towards the divine, the higher.

From these early lines of Matthew's Gospel, I have outlined for us the primary foundational task—or duty—of the Christian. To awaken. But what in the world does this exactly mean? Here we can turn again to lines 20–24 of Matthew, and ultimately the decision Joseph has to make, and how it can allow us to understand what it is to 'awaken' both spiritually, and logically.

'But while he thought on these things'—Joseph is in thought—in the pre-Christian act of thought—and then an angel of the Lord appears to him. The angel explains the situation, and Joseph, no longer described to be 'in thought' or thinking, rises from his 'sleep', and carries out that which has been commanded. In short, what can we say is happening here when abstracted down to a matter of events? Joseph is presented with reality, and he accepts it as it is and thus is taken/takes himself *up* from his sleep. I am reminded here of one of my favourite quotations from Anthony Wilden—'Reality is what trips you up when you don't pay attention to it'.

In literal sleep (snoozing in bed for eight hours every night), we enter into a world of fantasy, or irreality, or dreams and wishes. In waking sleep, these same forms of irreality exist, and yet we are conscious enough to justify them, to peddle them, to mould them to our surroundings. As we walk through our lives ignoring the immediate facts before us ... within us, we consistently *develop* (false) reasons as to why that which we daydream is so. We are muddled up in the lower levels of being, and the first call from the Gospels, and thus from Above (from the angel sent by the Lord) is to wake up, is to rise *up*, is to—as Aquinas might say—reach upward towards the *fullness of being*, toward all that one can be.

A digression: God −>Angels −> Humans −> Animals −> Plants −> Rocks. The Great Chain of Being, which, from afar, seems a little too straightforward, a little atomised and didactic. But it is a focus on that latter word which is of the most importance here, of *being*. *To be* is a state in which one (roughly speaking) has the greatest intensity of experiential reality in relation to that which is True (the Truth also being the Good), and thus the higher up the Great Chain of Being one goes, the greater the Being and therefore the greater the Truth. (Arguably God is *beyond* this as He *created* Being itself, or a different case altogether, though I haven't time for that here). And thus, the lower down the chain one goes, the lower the being, the less intense, one could even say, the more ontologically anhedonic or apathetic one is, to the point of nothingness.

But equally, within each iteration/level of this chain, one can quite as easily unfold that level into multiple minor levels. Most certainly, some animals have a greater fullness of being than others, as—I imagine—do some plants. For humans such an idea is undebatable, there are multiple *states* of *being* when it comes to being a human, many of which we go through each day. We sleep in the usual manner, awake into a daydream hazy fog, become a little more conscious and attentive, and then we reverse these states until bedtime. Perhaps a few of us enter into meditation, silence, and possibly even contemplation. And between all these states, it is undoubtedly that there are clear differences in being. So what is it then that we are being asked to do—as Joseph was—in the first passage (after the lineage) within the Gospel of Matthew? We are being asked to 'wake/rise up', which is to say 'ascend' the Chain of Being as much as possible, which is to say 'become conscious' of the Grace of existence (Being) itself which has been given to us *as* granted, and yet we take *for* granted, and it is in this difference where the lesson finds its turbulent conclusion.

If we are to take our being—our existence and potential to *be* conscious—*for* granted, then we take it in a possessive and presumptive manner, whereby it's a matter of fact that we have 'it', and 'it' doesn't exist within a spectrum (itself implying a hierarchy and the notion of superiority, God as both ontologically Above and morally above, etc). When we take being *for* granted we ignore it, we don't *work* out its spiritual potentiality (*'You see that a man is justified by works and not by faith alone'* (James 2:24))

However, what we are being asked to *do* in this earlier passage in Matthew is to *be*, whereby *being* consists in acknowledgement of something which has been given *as* granted by God from above (to *rise* up), and thus must be looked after, protected, healed, humbled, and kept in fear, trembling, and obeyance. To 'rise up' is simultaneously to respect one's Being as a given Grace from God, to admit and adhere to the hierarchy of Being inherent within the universe, and, with regard to 'works', to remain conscious of the potentiality of being to increase, to intensify, and to ascend vertically.

So for now we understand—to a very rough degree—what our task is as individual Christians, who is this figure Jesus Christ who it is we are to awaken for? Well once more we need only to turn to St Matthew's Gospel and delve deep:

> [1] *When Jesus therefore was born in Bethlehem of Juda, in the days of king Herod, behold, there came wise men from the east to Jerusalem.*
>
> [2] *Saying, Where is he that is born king of the Jews? For we have seen his star in the east, and are come to adore him.*
>
> (Matthew 2:1–2)

Once again we find two sections of narrative with little to anchor us with regard to what is truly happening. And yet, it is there. The emphasis I would place on these excerpts from Matthew would be on the words *Bethlehem* and *star*, both having a strange connection regarding astronomical, geographical, and symbolic rights and legitimacy. Within these two lines, Jesus Christ's authority is all at once told, shown, and—possibly—understood by us.

Bethlehem we are told—in Luke 2:4—is *'the city of David'*, a connection which already loops us back to the beginning of Matthew, to the begets, to the genealogical *authority* of Jesus. And so not only are we at first *told*, via the Word, of Christ's authority, but we are now—doubly so—*shown* of it via the events themselves. Jesus' birth within this 'city of David' is a twofold act of symbolic expression, it shows both his position and purpose. First we are to understand that his position is one of authority, as a birth resulting from the Davidic line. And second, Bethlehem in Hebrew (*Bet Lehem*) means 'house of bread'—and so as to Jesus' purpose we have a clue, for bread is that which nourishes us, quenches our hunger, is created from a grain (a seed), and ultimately becomes the supreme gift from God—*'Take this and eat, for this is my body'*. And so in short we see two clear statements with regard to Jesus' birth in Bethlehem: He is here to nourish us, *and* he is authorised to do so.

This notion of authority is shown to us equally with the arrival of the *'star in the east'*. It is of note that it is not just 'a' star, but 'his' star. This star also recalls a prophecy from the Book of Numbers, as Balaam predicted: *'a star shall come forth out of Jacob, and a sceptre shall rise out of Israel'* (Numbers 24:17). So first we have the symbol of bread, and of bread *as nourishment*, therefore we understand that Jesus has arrived to nourish; and now, connected to a prophecy foretold in the Old Testament, we have the symbol of the sceptre. The sceptre represents both the vertical and authority in general—*'Your throne, O God, will last for ever and ever; a sceptre of justice will be the sceptre of your kingdom'* (Hebrews 1:8). So, not only has Jesus arrived to nourish and heal, but he is also doubly *authorised* to do so. There is more here, enough to give an overview of the horizontal and the vertical, that is, The Cross.

I seek to explain the symbolism of the Cross via the 'star' from the east. Now, oddly enough, very little has been written about this star, with most modern commentators bowing down to modern science and seeking to *prove* that this star was there at all. The very same people would likely miss such a star by looking at the finger pointing at it. It clearly is not the matter of a 'material star' being in X place at Y time which is of importance, itself a 'horizontal' phenomenon. It is the star's vertical importance that matters. And so, what are these terms of the 'horizontal' and the 'vertical'? Well, as one can imagine, the former is that which visually sits on the 'left/right' axis (a horizontal line), and the vertical is that which visually sits on the above/below—'up/down' axis (a vertical line). But looking at both of these terms in this manner ironically subsumes both into the domain of the horizontal (the world, the linear).

To understand these terms, at first, we must look at both via the lens of temporality, of time. When we think of a horizontal line, a line that is on the left/right axis—or even the left-to-right axis—we can visualise the phenomenon of temporal progress as we commonly experience it. That is to say, our lives are a horizontal line in time that progresses from birth, through adolescence, to adulthood, into old age, and finally arrives at death. An experience caught between the two poles of birth and death, or, in the words of Nabakov: 'Life is just one small piece of light between two eternal darknesses'.

The horizontal is that which encapsulates—quite literally—our material existence here on earth: it is the past, the present, and the future; it is time marching on. Many people get caught up in time, get caught up in *one* kind of time. They believe that the past will always be as it 'was', the present is merely a fleeting moment never grasped, and the future is that which draws us to our end. Such people often attempt to find ways *within* this form of time to help them forget about this form of time. What do I mean by this? The 'fruits' of linear, horizontal time shall always rot, for they are beholden to the ticking of the clock; they are beholden to suffering, decay, and eventually death. And so the escapes which are found within the linear can never overcome the linear; an exotic holiday will always have an end; a delicious meal has to be finished; it is mandatory for the party to have its hangover—one cannot escape the passing of time via further dressed-up passing. Lying down flat as man does amidst the collapse of the horizontal, the answer he seeks is found in the act of standing, in the act of rising up (as we saw with the case of Joseph).

The vertical is something different altogether. It is a symbol of our relationship with God, and thus are potential of being and for being.

At the foot of the Cross one is looking *up* at the vertical;—looking up at God with a feeling of awe. We reach for heaven, and as we do He extends His mercy and grace down upon us. The vertical is the aforementioned sceptre prophesised in Numbers by the arrival of 'his' star. And so with the arrival of the star comes the arrival of legitimacy from above, authority from above. The acts of this child, of Jesus, are divinely authorised. His nourishment is *just*. But the vertical has a great, mirrored *meaning* for man. In fact, one could say, it is the quality *of* meaning for man.

Whereas the horizontal is the line from which man *must* set forward into the future, into likely suffering, and ultimately death. The vertical is that which intersects with the horizontal to give the existence of the momentary present its intensity of being. In each moment man must, by the very reality of existence, exist within the horizontal passing of time. Yet it is entirely his choice in each moment to *open* himself to the vertical. To open himself to all that is spiritual and divine, to all that which is offered to him from above as granted. In relation to time, it is to understand that in any given (horizontal) present, one truly has the capacity to reach into the eternal—what they will find there, or hear there, I cannot say. But so too, in each present, is each given the opportunity to exist in pure internal silence, and *open* themselves to eternity and God. It is not, then, that the vertical of the Cross is found at some point *later* in time, but the possibility of a relationship with the vertical can be nowhere but the present, for the past and the future do not exist. Ergo, God, as fount of all being, is with us at all times.

Not only then do we find in these passages clear symbolism of the horizontal and the vertical, and how they combine to create an authoritative act of the divine. Equally, we find that one can *read* the Gospels in a horizontal manner—the 'star' is just a star—and thus turn away from the beauty of the vertical. And yet, both are needed together. If one is solely horizontal, one is a man entirely *of* the world, all is material, all is matter, all is ... flat. If one is solely of the vertical, one is a man entirely *out of* the world, all is ethereal, all is 'divine, all is ... uncertain'. This latter state might seem ideal, and yet one must accept their reality, their place on earth, whilst simultaneously accepting their *internal* propensity for the Kingdom of God. Feet on the ground, heart in the heavens.

Another key passage, that even those of you who had the basic form of education regarding Christianity I mentioned at the beginning of the book will understand, is that of Jesus' temptation in the desert, usually known simply as 'The Temptation of Jesus', I will place it here in full as to analyse it:

> *¹ Then Jesus was led by the spirit into the desert, to be tempted by the devil.*
>
> *² And when he had fasted forty days and forty nights, afterwards he was hungry.*
>
> *³ And the tempter coming said to him: If thou be the Son of God, command that these stones be made bread.*
>
> *⁴ Who answered and said: It is written, Not in bread alone doth man live, but in every word that proceedeth from the mouth of God.*
>
> *⁵ Then the devil took him up into the holy city, and set him upon the pinnacle of the temple.*
>
> *⁶ And said to him: If thou be the Son of God, cast thyself down, for it is written: That he hath given his angels charge over thee, and in their hands shall they bear thee up, lest perhaps thou dash thy foot against a stone.*
>
> *⁷ Jesus said to him: It is written again: Thou shalt not tempt the Lord thy God.*
>
> *⁸ Again the devil took him up into a very high mountain, and shewed him all the kingdoms of the world, and the glory of them.*
>
> *⁹ And said to him: All these will I give thee, if falling down thou wilt adore me.*
>
> *¹⁰ Then Jesus saith to him: Begone, Satan: for it is written, The Lord thy God shalt thou adore, and him only shalt thou serve.*
>
> *¹¹ Then the devil left him; and behold angels came and ministered to him.*
>
> (Matthew 4:1–11)

First and foremost one might ask 'Well if Jesus was (and is) so powerful, why was it that He was tempted at all?' There are a couple of answers to this, one basic and one deeply spiritual. In the most basic sense, we understand that Jesus was both *fully* man and *fully* God. As such, being fully man, Jesus was therefore human as much as the rest of us and open to the reality of temptation, that is, open to the struggle in relation to the decision between what is wrong and what is right. Though this answer is theologically satisfying, it's not necessarily spiritually or personally satisfying because it doesn't quite answer the question of *why* temptation needs to be at all and what Jesus' response to temptation teaches us about what it is to *be* a Christian.

Much like loving God, or love in its most general sense, the notion of virtue has to arise from a decision for it to mean anything at all. If there is no choice, no struggle, or even no agency involved then what could we say of one's actions? An action that is Good is definitely Good in itself, but if the person undertaking the action was forced to do so, we might struggle to define whether or not they themselves are a good person. Likewise, without the decision from faith to love God and receive His grace, what could be said of our relationship with Him? If we were *made* to love Him without a choice in the matter we could no longer say this was love. What I'm talking about here is friction.

Ask yourself how it is you would get to the other side of the room you're now in. I imagine you would walk (or push yourself if within a wheelchair). And how exactly do these actions get underway? The answer is friction. Our feet have to *push* against the ground, our bodies have to withstand gravity, and we have to balance ourselves against thousands of different things that have long-since become second nature. But at a certain point in time, when we were all tiny, we had to learn to walk. Or, we had to learn to work with friction. This is all very well but what does it have to do with temptation? Everything. Imagine if you will that your floor is now the most perfect sheet of ice and there isn't anything at all to hold onto. You would try to push and move but without friction, you would end up nowhere, this is a metaphorical version of what 'love' would look like if it was forced. The same applies to Jesus and ourselves, without some struggle against the friction of the world, we cannot truly say we have been tempted or overcome that which holds us back from a greater relationship with God.

In preparation for this temptation—the desert being a symbol of a place without life to sustain us—Jesus fasts for 40 days, rids Himself of anything worldly as sustenance, and relies solely on the Grace of God to get Him through. And so it begins: *'If thou be the Son of God, command that these stones be made bread'* (Matthew 4:3).

At this juncture, Jesus is unimaginably hungry after not eating for 40 days, and the first temptation—or the first purification, a term I will get to later—is targeted at the most worldly and material of desires, that of food. Yet there is far more depth to this saying than one first realises. This first temptation that Jesus is asked to perform is both a temptation of God (as all the temptations are), in that it seeks to *prove* God/Jesus' greatness by way of material theatrics, whilst simultaneously being a bastardisation of those powers by seeking to drag the heavens down to earth. For Jesus is not asked to perform anything implicitly spiritual, but simply to transform one form of the world into another form of the world, stones into bread. This 'bread' therein, is both a foreshadowing and twisted play on the latter Bread that *is* the body of Christ. The devil herein seeks to tempt, foul, and immanentise God's powers to bolster the world. Jesus replies 'Not in bread alone doth man live, but in every word that proceedeth from the mouth of God', so as to say that no amount of such material/worldly bolstering can amount to the Grace of the divine. To live by the former bread of the devil would be to give oneself over entirely to the world.

Next, the devil asks Jesus to take Himself to the pinnacle of the temple, a platform some 450 feet high, and throw Himself off, in the knowledge that angels (under His command) shall catch Him. Jesus replies by stating *'Thou shalt not tempt the Lord thy God'*. That life, as that which is *of* the Creator *as* Creation is thus His to command and carry, and to test the Lord in this way is to distrust His omnipresent judgement.

Finally, the devil takes Jesus to a very high mountain—once again emphasising that this is a worldly height—and offers Him all the kingdoms of the world (the devil's domain), to which Jesus replies *'Begone, Satan: for it is written, The Lord thy God shalt thou adore, and him only shalt thou serve'*. For the world is only *all* that is lower, and even in its enormity is still nothing but the aforementioned worldly 'bread' when compared with the Grace of the Lord. Yet it is the next line that I think is of the utmost importance here, and the one from which we as individuals can understand how temptation and friction become synonymous. 'Then the devil left him; and behold angels came and ministered to him'. Notice that this is a single line and not two separate events without correlation. The devil (and temptation) leaving Jesus is inherently related to the coming and ministry of the angels. This is why I mentioned the notion of *purification* in relation to temptation earlier on. Jesus was clearing away vice and sin to make *space* for virtue and grace. As darkness and light cannot coexist, neither too can virtue and vice. So, much like a spoiled garden that holds the promise of greatness, Jesus was first dealing with the weeds and bad soil before planting anything. For any seed thrown into an untended garden will quickly be forgotten. This same metaphor can be expanded into the realm of friction already mentioned. If we imagine a garden with already-given perfect soil, perfect sunlight, and perfectly timed rain, can we in any sense call the man who tends it a gardener? I don't believe so. But the man who spends his life quietly tending his garden, uprooting weeds, cutting away the chaff, noticing rocks and knots, paying attention to that which needs to be cut away, and expends his own energy watering and catering to his plants (his soul's) needs, now this man we can call a gardener. And so it is that in just a few lines Jesus—via the Gospels—affords us the archetypal, macrocosmic story of how it is God deals with temptation to allow us—His image—a means of understanding how to attend to our own.

Jesus recruits disciples

[13] And going up into a mountain, he called unto him whom he would himself: and they came to him.

[14] And he made that twelve should be with him, and that he might send them to preach.

[15] And he gave them power to heal sicknesses, and to cast out devils.

[16] And to Simon he gave the name Peter:

[17] And James the son of Zebedee, and John the brother of James; and he named them Boanerges, which is, The sons of thunder:

[18] And Andrew and Philip, and Bartholomew and Matthew, and Thomas and James of Alpheus, and Thaddeus, and Simon the Cananean:

[19] And Judas Iscariot, who also betrayed him.

(Mark 3:13–19)

With the 12 Disciples, we once again have a piece of knowledge so common to our culture that we rarely stop to think about it. Who were these disciples? Why were they chosen? What were they like? Why was there 12? Okay, let's get that last one out of the way because it's the simplest. There were 12 disciples chosen by Jesus because 12 represented the 12 tribes of Israel (God's chosen people) in the Old Testament. In fact, the disciples as both a reality and an idea we can draw into our own lives are all about *choice* and *decision*.

First we see that Jesus 'called unto him' the 12 who were to be His Disciples. That is to say—and as the local bishop told each person individually at my Rite of the Elect—Jesus has chosen *you*. He wants you. You have been called. It is a feeling like no other, that, speaking transparently, pulls you this way and that and before you know it you're standing somewhere you never foresaw, with people you never imagined you would be shoulder-to-shoulder with.

But herein, before the Crucifixion and thus prior to the moment of mankind's redemption, who is it that Jesus is choosing? For within this choice, we perceive a mirror as to the other side of Christ's death on the Cross wherein we all can be saved, wherein we all can be chosen and thus choose to be His followers. And so who is it that is chosen at first? Is it men of great power such as merchants and kings? Is it those who have in some sense already proven their moral/pious worth? Not at all. Those who are chosen are as they are. They are fallible human beings, and in this way become extremely relatable. Whether it's Peter's doubt, John's fiery nature, or even the silence of Simon (we know almost nothing about him), one can see that those chosen by Jesus are not somehow special or different in nature. In fact, they are those who are consistently self-aware of their all-too-human nature and yet continue in their attempts to imitate Jesus anyway. Even in their (universally human) weakness, they responded to Jesus' call with a 'Yes'. The Disciples, then, are those who repeatedly pick themselves back up when fall down.

After the call, however, comes the work. What exactly is it these disciples are to do? As we can see from the Gospel, they are to preach, heal, or cast out devils. This is to say that they are chosen and appointed to a vocation of sorts. The very action of accepting Jesus' call begets some form of stability, even if it is just to be with Him and hold to Him in faith. Throughout this quite sparse Gospel passage, there is a noticeable lack of rationale or reason. There are no reasons as to why each disciple heeded the call other than those each found in their heart. This in itself is some of the best, hidden advice this passage of Scripture has to offer. Namely, don't worry about whether it makes sense *to* you, concern yourself with whether or not it makes sense *to* you. For in following this call you now set out down a path that shall give your life direction and purpose, even if at times this direction is amidst uncertainty.

Yet even amidst this path one has been called to follow, there are more details within just this Gospel passage that will allow us to understand our place within the world. First, the 12 Disciples are sent out *to preach*. One can read this as spreading the Word of God, though to the ears of a former atheist, this notion still brings forth images of dry lectures, dogmatics, and excessive *thou shalt nots*. This is why allowing the call of Christ to make sense *of* you is so important, for in that understanding preaching is transformed into one's being. The proclamations of one's very person, the way they are what they do, are the preaching itself. That is, the Word of God is largely a description of actions to be lived as opposed to the theory to be studied. Going out into the world to preach is to go out into the world and *be* Christian. For there is a stark difference between teaching what it is to be charitable and actually being charitable.

Following this, the Disciples were called to *heal*, and though post-crucifixion individuals are not necessarily called to heal in the sense of healing hands, we are called to heal in the etymological sense of *making another whole*. Helping them hear the call and leading them towards that which we understand will in time make sense to them. And finally, the disciples are called to *cast out devils*. Are we to understand from this that we Christians are to go out to perform exorcisms? Absolutely not. We are to understand that in casting something out we therein prioritise the good (as with Jesus' temptations in the desert).

Yet, there is that mysterious sentence here at the end of this Gospel passage, wherein after the names of 11 of the disciples, we are told Jesus also calls '*Judas Iscariot, who also betrayed him*'. We find here the mystery of Jesus consciously calling and choosing someone whom He knew would eventually betray Him, thereby leading to His death on the Cross. What are we to make of this? Well, on the one hand, I cannot do this passage theological justice because it has been one of the great talking points of Scripture for centuries. On the other hand, drawing out from Jesus' decision that which one can use, we understand that even in the face of the most outrageous betrayal and denial (knowingly from both Peter and Judas), Jesus is eternally and infinitely forgiving. The onus is on the human being regarding their response to infinite love. Are they going to accept that love can be infinite and repent despite their betrayal (in the case of Peter)? Or are they going to double down on the world and take matters into their own hands (in the case of Judas)? The decision is one of pride. Are we as fallible human beings truly going to believe that we have one up on the Creator, or are we going to humble ourselves as creation and open ourselves to love and forgiveness?

* * *

Exercise 3

This exercise is just as simple as the previous two, it is a single walk.

Before undertaking this walk sit for a few minutes and quiet your thoughts.

Find the time to go for a 30–60-minute walk, preferably somewhere peaceful where one can at least somewhat quieten their mind. As you walk, meditate on what you happen to see. From trees to buildings, other people to animals, think about where each thing came from, how it got here, and what helped it get here. Don't force the answers, if there is no clear cause then simply accept that. Meditate also on how everything communicates, what things rely on other things, and, how everything is connected.

If you wish to extend this exercise, then do this same walk every day for a week.

Journal your findings.

* * *

The Sermon on the Mount

But what of Jesus' actual teaching? It's common to hear retorts targeted at Christian *institutions* that they have misinterpreted or in some sense mutated the teachings of Jesus Himself. Almost always these sorts of debates regarding the 'correct' reading of a certain piece of Scripture end in little more than name-calling and hatred (from both sides). Ironically, then, most efforts to defend Christianity result in falling further away from Christ than when they first started, giving themselves over to the world and to power.

So let us turn to Jesus' Sermon on the Mount, that passage wherein He gives us eight relatively simple pieces of advice, that when contemplated open up into an infinite wealth of wisdom. Commonly known as the Beatitudes, the passage from the Gospel of Matthew is as follows:

> *[1] And seeing the multitudes, he went up into a mountain, and when he was set down, his disciples came unto him.*
>
> *[2] And opening his mouth, he taught them, saying:*
>
> *[3] Blessed are the poor in spirit: for theirs is the kingdom of heaven.*
>
> *[4] Blessed are the meek: for they shall possess the land.*
>
> *[5] Blessed are they that mourn: for they shall be comforted.*
>
> *[6] Blessed are they that hunger and thirst after justice: for they shall have their fill.*
>
> *[7] Blessed are the merciful: for they shall obtain mercy.*
>
> *[8] Blessed are the clean of heart: for they shall see God.*

> [9] *Blessed are the peacemakers: for they shall be called children of God.*
> [10] *Blessed are they that suffer persecution for justice' sake: for theirs is the kingdom of heaven.*
> [11] *Blessed are ye when they shall revile you, and persecute you, and speak all that is evil against you, untruly, for my sake.*
>
> (Matthew 5:1–12)

Herein it's always worth reserving some attention to the fact that from the Christian perspective, we are not merely attempting to understand some arbitrary guidelines to make our worldly lives easier, but are seeking to understand the Words of the Lord as they were literally spoken by Him here on earth. This is not a matter of a philosophical, highly theoretical lecture on ethics, but a Sermon by God on what it is to *be* a pious and loving individual. It is also worth focusing on the fact that each Beatitude is structured with a former *condition* and a latter *result*. For instance, the result of receiving the Kingdom of Heaven is via the condition of being poor in spirit, and so on.

Though I tackle the first Beatitude in greater depth later on in the section on silence and humility, it does, however, begin a common trend across the entirety of the Beatitudes, that of a historically contextual inversion of what it is to be blessed. It is not the rich, the powerful, the rulers, or the kings who are blessed, but the poor, the meek, the merciful, and the peacemakers. Jesus' Sermon on the Mount, proclaimed before the masses, is foremost simply radical. Adhering to a radicality that many still struggle to understand in its simplicity. So not only is Jesus teaching it isn't rulers, kings, and the rich who are blessed (by the fact of their apparent riches as somehow proof of blessing), but via the inversion of these values is opening up the gateway to God to *all*, even the most wretched, lowly, and poor person. Alongside this general acknowledgement underlying the Beatitudes in their entirety is the first declaration that the Kingdom of Heaven is not for those who are poor in spirit, those who are *not* secure in their faith and salvation, but in fact those who humble themselves in their uncertainty and consistently strive despite acknowledgement of their sinful nature.

However, let us turn to the meek. The meek are those who are mild, kind, and gentle. It is the opposite of pride. The meek are the creations that humble themselves before the Creator. Within the modern world, however, meekness is commonly conflated with weakness, but this is far from reality. For the meek are not pushovers, they are those who have accepted that the world in all its materiality has nothing to offer them that can compare with the delights of heaven and of salvation. There is a quote by Meister Eckhart (2009):

> The only thing that burns in hell is the part of you that won't let go of your life: your memories, your attachments. They burn them all away, but they're not punishing you, they're freeing your soul. If you're frightened of dying and you're holding on, you'll see devils tearing your life away. If you've made your peace, then the devils are really angels freeing you from the earth.

And such is the case between meekness and pride. The meek, in their kindness and acceptance of God's love, will feel no need to cling to anything of this world and seek only to help other men (other creations) within this life from a position of openness and human love. Inversely, the prideful cling to this life as if they are not merely creation, but believe themselves to be Creator, and therefore cling to what they believe is rightfully theirs. And so it is that we find within the second Beatitude an odd paradox, wherein those who do not cling to the land in an act of immanent, false ownership, find themselves to be the one possessing the land of heaven. It all seems abstract, but one needs to focus on just how quickly life manages to pass us by, confirming the realisation that no act of clinging or grasping will ever amount to anything, for one can only hold onto something for as long as they live and that happens to not be all that long. Kindness, gentleness, and love, however, are the opposite of grasping and therein spread themselves into life long after one has left this world for the next.

Yet with this openness also comes an inward openness. For our relationship with God is reciprocal, and the more we understand of ourselves the more we understand of God and vice versa. Leading us to the next Beatitude, one that is—unsurprisingly—overlooked: *'Blessed are they that mourn: for they shall be comforted'*. Our contemporary conception of mourning tends to stop at funerals and the death of loved ones, beyond this we are likely reluctant to mourn anything else. Yet following those who are *poor in spirit* and those who are *meek* we can surmise that the Beatitudes are at most only secondarily related to the world, and in the sense that they are it is such that it is in a manner of forgetting. So even though it is that God shall comfort us during our trials and worldly mournings amidst loss and suffering, this is not the mourning that Jesus is talking about here.

He is speaking about spiritual mourning. For as we express sorrow and distress during a funeral, so too should we seek to experience such in relation to our own failures, sins, and weaknesses. Within this mourning then, this grief targeted at our own inner world, we are moving beyond ourselves towards a greater relationship with God. Let us, in fact, mirror these two forms of mourning to understand the difference.

First we have worldly mourning, wherein within the days, weeks, months, and years after the loss of a loved one we experience a feeling of sorrow at the knowledge and understanding that we will never see them again. And yet, within that mourning needs to come a point of maturity. For one cannot simply lie down and die with the person and allow the mourning itself to overcome them, as if life has stopped for them and them alone. As such, within the experience of mourning, one needs to form a new relationship with the world that draws the best from their previous experience, brings it into the present, and allows them to transform the situation (to the best of their ability and strength) to the betterment of all.

We can now mirror this form of worldly mourning and spiritually transmute it in relation to the Beatitude in question. When we mourn our sins and failures, those times when we know we could have done and *been* better, we may allow ourselves a few days to wallow in guilt, justification, or stress. But anyone who has been around a little while knows that after a short while this does no good at all, in fact, it does the inverse and ends up simply swallowing a person's finite time into nothing. And so what one now needs to do with that experience of mourning (grief, sorrow) is repent. But not repent in the stereotypical modern sense wherein one is kneeling in the town square bellowing an apology to the heavens but in the etymological sense of *metanoia*.

Metanoia, meaning literally repentance or penance (though it loses its nuance in the literal sense), is formed of *meta* (to change) and *noia* (from *noein* and *nous*, meaning mind). To repent, then, is to change one's mind. Though that subverts the whole thing back to modern English and makes it rather flat. I like to think of it as a *metamorphosis of being*, wherein the change we are to undertake is intent on transforming ourselves in such a way that the failure shall be no more, and the mind (*nous*) that will make this change is our own.

So, in a very roundabout fashion, taking a detour through the most abused word in the Christian dictionary—Repent!—we come to understand that those who mourn are blessed because via their mourning they are prepared to change their very being towards God and Jesus in much the same way one who mourns the dead must change themselves towards the betterment of all after acknowledgement of loss. The comfort that is afforded those who mourn is both from their own working through their sins and, simultaneously, the act of feeling closer to God via the act of mourning and *metanoia*.

But this doesn't quite cover why the word *mourning* evokes a certain feeling within us. There is pain within that word, this is not just a case of being sorry and trying to change, it is something more. What is missing in this discussion then is what or who we are mourning? For now, we can retrospectively understand why Jesus spoke of mourning and not something else. As we mourn our sins, we inherently mourn His death, for He died for our sins and for our redemption. Though we have possibly failed ourselves, our families, and our communities via our sins and faults, the sting of mourning is in the acknowledgement that our moral transgressions have already been paid for by the blood of Christ, and so each trespass feels as an extra insult to the Creator. Those who mourn are blessed because their reverence is an ever-present twofold acceptance of sin *and* forgiveness; fault *and* love; trespass *and* salvation. Our hearts cry out in mourning to He who has *already* forgiven us.

This mourning, however, equally begets an internal sense of haste and striving. Via our mourning we come to understand our innate fallen nature, our fallibility, and our sin, from this, we come to desire and love He who can lead us from this state of being even more. As such, the third Beatitude leads directly into the fourth: *'Blessed are they that hunger and thirst after justice: for they shall have their fill'*. Hunger and thirst therein are states of urgency, for when one is truly hungry or thirsty one would do almost anything to quench those feelings. This applies equally in the spiritual sense, wherein one who mourns their sin and becomes spiritually hungry and thirsty heeds a call to drop as much as they can to move towards God more fully. Therefore 'justice' (or 'righteousness' in other translations) *is* the definition of one's relationship with God. It is this ongoing relationship with the Lord that will allow us our 'fill', satisfying us. These first four Beatitudes can be collected together and understood as teaching us the need to *be* a disciple and therefore needing something higher than ourselves (God the Father) to help us in our spiritual journey. Our own efforts alone cannot suffice to bring us contentment.

However, as the first four Beatitudes *poor in spirit, meekness, mourning,* and *hunger* are regarding our relationship to the Lord and how we are to comport ourselves towards Him, the last four—*mercy, clean heart, peace-making,* and *suffering*—are in relation to what *we*, as individuals can do to receive further blessings from God, and as such are much simpler, as they all relate to relatively clear and concise actions that are well within the power of all to undertake and spread throughout the world.

Beginning with, *'Blessed are the merciful: for they shall obtain mercy'*, a statement we see mirrored in the Lord's Prayer with *'Forgive us our debts, as we also have forgiven our debtors'* (Matthew 6:12) This is one of the Beatitudes that I don't think needs much exposition. We need to show love and compassion to those in need and in turn the Lord will show us love and compassion. Love, mercy, and forgiveness (all of which are to some degree interchangeable) are the Lord's key traits, and so in enacting them throughout the world, we draw ourselves closer to God by understanding how *He* loves His creation.

Mercy itself, as a trait, is found within the next Beatitude, *'Blessed are the clean of heart: for they shall see God'*. Note that 'clean' here is often translated as 'pure', though both attend to the notion already mentioned of the heart as a garden and the first thing one must do if they wish to grow fruits—for we shall know them by their fruits—is to clear away the metaphorical weeds and rocks. A pure heart, then, is one that is without hatred, malice, jealousy, greed, or any of the other worldly graspings that make us feel as if we should place ourselves higher than another. As such, purity is inherently something else *other* than the world due to the world's fallen nature. Those who are pure of heart are therefore primarily moving themselves towards God throughout all things. After such purity is founded and held (through many ups and downs), it is such that one would bring their fruits into the world, becoming something of a 'peacemaker'. For we are told, *'Blessed are the peacemakers: for they shall be called children of God'*. As one can imagine, this is very much a case wherein one brings joy, love, and peace to the world. Once again this reflects God's mercy towards His creation.

And finally, we have *'Blessed are they that suffer persecution for justice' sake: for theirs is the kingdom of heaven'*. Connected to the prior three Beatitudes most thoroughly (though all are related), we now understand what it is to be with and under God, and also how to act *for* God.

This final Beatitude, however, outlines the result for those who are pure of heart and peacemakers who hold fast to their faith in the Lord throughout trials where they will be persecuted. We once again see a mirroring between the teaching of this Beatitude and the eventual fate of Christ, wherein He suffered for His beliefs on the Cross. The final section of Christ's life is known as 'the Passion'.

* * *

Exercise 4

Before undertaking this exercise sit for a few minutes and calm your thoughts.

Reread the passage from the Sermon on the Mount above (Matthew 5:1–12), go through each Beatitude individually, spending five minutes meditating on each, and ask yourself whether or not you agree with my analysis. Perform these meditations on separate days if you feel you need to. Then meditate on the image of Jesus (the Son of God/God Himself) talking to a crowd from the Mount.

Ask yourself what it means to be a good person.

Ask yourself why it is often so difficult to perform the most basic acts of kindness and charity.

Ask yourself why you think it is that human beings continue to be so cruel to one another in light of the Beatitudes.

Ask yourself why cruelty, war, and hatred between human beings have never truly ceased.

Journal your findings.

* * *

The passion

Let's continue with the Life of Jesus Christ and look at how it ends. The Passion of the Christ for many people, especially the secular and underinformed, may easily be conflated with the 2004 film of that exact name, therein missing the key separation within the title between 'the Passion' and 'of the Christ'. The Passion is itself understood as the narrative wherein Christ gave His final instructions, was denied by Peter, underwent the Agony in the Garden of Gethsemane, was arrested and tried under Pontius Pilate, was Crucified, died, buried, and then rose from the dead. It is the narrative that's most familiar to us, at least the Crucifixion event.

Very few, it seems, actually know what it means or why it's of such importance. It's common knowledge that a man named Jesus died on the Cross. It might be known that in doing so, He died for our sins. Beyond this, one hears little of the meaning of these events, with them often being subsumed into the common culture as just another famous image among images. For many, Christ upon the Cross has become little more than a mass-produced necklace one wears as a fashion accessory or mainstay of knowledge. Rarely do we stop and reflect on the symbol and its deeper meaning.

Passion, coming from the Latin *patior* refers to suffering, enduring, and/or bearing. The Passion, then, is that event unto which Christ suffered the utmost of all humiliations and tortures, crucifixion. At first glance, it would appear that one would undergo such punishment because of crimes they committed as one does a jail sentence, it would be peculiar to ask, 'What does this punishment mean?', and yet in the case of Jesus Christ we must, for within its meaning lies the understanding of our own redemption and possibility for peace.

The Bible, as read from the Old Testament through to the New Testament, almost entirely holds a rupture in the fabric of being, something disharmonious, the original wrong which must be righted for all to be well again. I am talking of Original Sin. Almost immediately man betrays the Lord and is cast out from Eden (a harmonious state where men walk alongside God), herein we reject God's love, and henceforth we would need a perfect form of love to right this wrong. The rejection which broke the unconditional love can only be healed by He who loves unconditionally—hence why God made Himself human in the God-man Jesus Christ. God, as Jesus, in His innocence took upon the guilt of all and paid the penalty humanity needed to pay. For if Jesus was not God, His death would not be able to redeem us, and the Crucifixion would be no more than any other routine Roman punishment.

Yet, Jesus was God, and He stated just prior to the Passion during the Last Supper:

> [26] *And whilst they were at supper, Jesus took bread, and blessed, and broke: and gave to his disciples, and said: Take ye, and eat. This is my body.*
>
> [27] *And taking the chalice, he gave thanks, and gave to them, saying: Drink ye all of this.*
>
> [28] *For this is my blood of the new testament, which shall be shed for many unto remission of sins.*
>
> (Matthew 26:26–28)

Thus, both instituting the Sacrament of the Eucharist and declaring that His body would be 'given up' upon the Cross and that His blood would be spilt upon the Cross for the forgiveness of our sins. The Passion is our *chance* at redemption; it is the moment wherein God's purpose for making Himself man comes to fruition, as to unconditionally forgive the original stain upon our souls and allow entry into the Kingdom.

This allowance, however, isn't necessarily unconditional with respect to our behaviour. It is not the case that post-Passion and after the Resurrection, one may simply do as they please and still gain the Kingdom. No, the gates which were once closed by Original Sin are now made open, but the choice as to whether or not one wishes to pass through this notably narrow gate is still theirs. For through this gate awaits God's perfect love, and yet being love means that He cannot force anyone to enter.

This reconciliation, this possibility of true forgiveness, and the possibility of *life everlasting* are made clear by the fact of the Resurrection. In rising from the dead we understand that Christ's *immortal* soul was reunited with an immortal body in such a place one can only call eternity. In rising from the world into the Kingdom, and 'returning' to appear and encounter others as the Risen Christ, we bear witness to the possible destination of the righteous. It shall be the Second Coming of Christ wherein all who had died shall be reunited in this manner.

In His death, Resurrection, and revelation, we bear witness to the fulfilment of prophecy as testified in the Old Testament in relation to that which barred us from Eden and the Kingdom (Original Sin), and therein Christ's Passion is that which truly set us free, as to be able to make the only choice which matters, between God and nothing, between the Lord and the world.

Yet rarely do we think about the immediate aftermath of Christ's Resurrection. What are we really left with, historically speaking? We have the peculiar events of Christ's life, His Words given over to many, and we have His disciples who sought to go forth and spread the new-found religion of Christianity (at that point simply 'Followers of Christ') throughout the world. But before it became the enormous—albeit fragmented—institutional religion it is today, what was needed for it to be solidified or understood as a religion? What are the basics that new followers of Christ would need to attend to so they could consider themselves Christians? I think one place to look for an answer to this question is the seven Sacraments. Though it took quite a while for the Sacraments to be accepted as seven (1215AD to be exact), they allow us a more didactic look at what the basic worldview of a Christian would come to look like in a practical sense. How is it we *become* a Christian? What are our *duties*? What of special occasions? The Sacraments, then, for myself, mark a clear move from the fragile end of the Life of Christ to the instalment of His Church within the world.

The Sacraments

Following the Life of Christ came St Paul and the beginnings of the *Christ*ian religion, that is, those who follow Jesus Christ. With this beginning equally arrived—over a short space of time—the institution of the Sacraments. There are seven Sacraments in total, each of which could be written (and has been written) volume after volume of commentary. Here I only seek to describe, later, in Part 2, I will draw them in as a way to expand upon the larger themes of Christian life. Please note that this book has a Catholic emphasis, not all denominations agree on the number of Sacraments or their exact meaning (the Eucharist, for instance, has an altered understanding among Protestants).

First up, and most importantly, we have Baptism. It is the Sacrament that frees man from Original Sin, makes him a member of Christ's Church, opens the doorway to the 'narrow path', and makes him a *New Man*. Baptism is necessary for salvation for it confers sanctifying graces and makes known our membership *in* Christ. To be Baptised is to have an irremovable mark placed upon one's eternal soul, a mark which metaphorically states I believe, I have faith, I am with Christ and His Church. It is administered by pouring natural water over someone's head whilst invoking the Holy Trinity—'*[Name], I baptise you in the name of the Father, and of the Son, and of the Holy Spirit*'. Baptism is beautifully simple and delicate, and yet its meaning is the opposite of trivial.

Next, we have the Sacrament of the Eucharist. Once again, a seemingly simple act of eating a small wafer and taking a sip of wine has folded into it sacrifice, Presence, and food for the faithful. The meaning of this Sacrament we can expand out from Scripture, specifically 1 Corinthians 11:25–27:

> *[25] In like manner also the chalice, after he had supped, saying: This chalice is the new testament in my blood: this do ye, as often as you shall drink, for the commemoration of me.*
> *[26] For as often as you shall eat this bread, and drink the chalice, you shall shew the death of the Lord, until he come.*
> *[27] Therefore whosoever shall eat this bread, or drink the chalice of the Lord unworthily, shall be guilty of the body and of the blood of the Lord.*

The Sacrament of the Eucharist declares Christ as our mediator with God, as He who is the one and only Son of God, and in being so is thus justified in His application of Nourishment to us via the Eucharist. In eating the Eucharist we are eating the *Risen* Body of Christ, for we believe in the act of Communion that the Real Presence of Christ is found and thus in eating *this bread* we are in truth sharing in Christ's sacrifice on the Cross, and in a sense 'spiritually nourishing' ourselves for the road ahead.

Next, we have the Sacrament of Confirmation. As it was—metaphorically—explained to me, before everything one has a divine spark within them. For their soul is *of* the divine or spiritual world, thus making men and women a type of 'bridge' between spirit and matter. In Baptism, it is as if kindling is added to our divine spark, and the fire of the Lord is made to rise within us. Confirmation, then (usually taking place at 14 years of age or older) is like fuel being poured atop the already present fire of God within us. It is the Sacrament of maturity; it is the full and knowing submission of our own will to Christ's. In this Sacrament, not only do we (externally) officially become members of the Catholic Church, but internally and symbolically, the Holy Spirit opens to us a full profession of faith. With the anointing of the blessed oil of chrism, one's faith is wilfully strengthened and thus determined to a life fully in consecration to the Lord.

As one is now—after these first three Sacraments—a full member and therein partaking in the life of the Church, it becomes a duty for those following Christ to constantly attempt to follow His Will, the Will of God. Of course, no human (not even the Pope) is perfect or infallible. We *will* make mistakes, we *will* end up sinning, and—whether intentionally or not—end up acting against the Will of God. Committing a sin is of course not good, however, one needs to remember that God *is* eternally and infinitely merciful and loving, and such a fact is almost of no use if one pretends to be perfect all the while. We are humans and we are constantly tripping up. The trick, however, isn't in trying to not trip up all the time, but in strengthening one's ability to get back up again and try some more to walk with Christ. The Sacrament of Penance, or the Sacrament of Confession, is a Sacramental aid in just that. The Church has the power to forgive all sins. This power is what was given from Christ (God) to the Apostles (John 20:21–23):

> [21] *Jesus said to them again, 'Peace be with you. As the Father has sent me, even so I send you'.*
> [22] *And when he had said this, he breathed on them, and said to them, 'Receive the Holy Spirit'.*
> [23] *'If you forgive the sins of any, they are forgiven; if you retain the sins of any, they are retained'.*

He then emphasised this as an individual act for our own forgiveness (1 John 1:9)

> *If we confess our sins, he is faithful and just and will forgive us our sins and purify us from all unrighteousness.*

Thus our Confession to a priest is therein in truth a Confession to Christ via those of His apostolic lineage who were given the power to forgive sins. Priests are not Christ but are acting in the capacity originally given to them by the Lord. The sinner must be contrite of heart. That is, the one who confesses must be truly remorseful within their heart if the Sacrament is to have an effect (see the earlier discussion on *metanoia*). It is a simple matter of asking a priest what you wish to confess, listing your sins, receiving penance (a prayer or action given by the priest in recognition of our sins), and then finally being granted absolution, wherein one's soul is clean again.

Next, we have a Sacrament that gets less acknowledgement than the others, but this may be because it's a little more morbid and one hears about it only on rare occasions. The Sacrament of Extreme Unction or Anointing of the Sick. This Sacrament 'removes that state which might be an obstacle to the clothing with the glory of the Resurrection' (www.catholic.org); it is given to the dying (or those who are thought to be dying at that moment) as a means to make them ready to enter upon the beatific vision (likely after a final Confession). It is ultimately a Sacrament to further give strength to those making their passage to the afterlife.

Next, we have the Sacrament of Holy Orders. Wherein four of the previous five Sacraments need to be given by a priest (Baptism can technically be performed by anyone, though a priest is preferable), one might ask how it is that one 'becomes' a priest. This is where the Sacrament of Holy Orders takes place via a bishop. As we have seen the mediatory function which Christ played—between heaven and earth; God and man—if it was to be continued needed legitimised mediators to continue it, thus was the duty and honour of the Apostles. In turn, the Apostles (and the 'Apostolic lineage') have been passed from priest to priest, bishop to bishop, thus continuing the line authorised by God Himself.

Finally, we have the Sacrament of Matrimony, or as most people know it, marriage. A spiritual contract between a man and a woman is thus raised by Christ and His Church to the dignity of a Sacrament. A true representation of Christ's sanctifying sacrifice and dedication to His Church is the reciprocal sacrifice and devotion of husband and wife. God has ordained marriage, and Christ elevated it to the status of a Sacrament. The marriage contract is a component of the Sacrament of Matrimony, making the two Christians inseparable.

Attended to in the manner I have here the Sacraments appear a little hasty, possibly even a little flat. I intended only an overview before going forward into the second half regarding the spirituality of Christianity, for their *worldly* practice is one-half of the story, and yet they can be thought of as those tools to which a Christian can turn to in times of distress. Therein they are tools for the soul, aids to help us on our journey through life, through the narrow path, and eventually into the afterlife.

The soul

But what is this relationship with God—that's being built via our participation in His Church and His Sacraments—helping or saving? What exactly are all these Sacraments and sacred tools for? The answer is one's soul. We can say that the end result of individual Christian action and virtue is help towards saving one's soul. As I mentioned at the start, the 'soul' is another elusive term that has made its way into the common tongue, often used in place of heart or depth. We might say that a piece of art touched one's soul, or that a certain undertaking is bad for one's soul. Modern man, then, still holds an innate understanding of Christian morality as the norm wherein good and evil are concerned. But the question we need to ask, before looking at how to *save* it, is what exactly *is* the soul?

The position of human beings is unique. We are not animals in the sense that they are made entirely of a 'body' or matter. We are not angels in the sense that they are made entirely of spirit. We are in-between, our existence is a mediation between spirit and matter, heaven and earth, the body and the soul. We are all well aware of what a body is, what our body is. For the body and the senses are brothers of a kind. Via the senses, we experience the majority of the world. We see, we hear, we touch, and we taste and smell all in relation to the body, they are bodily—matter-based—senses and experiences. Yet, when we die, our body alone will return to dust and another 'part' of us shall live on. For the soul is eternal, and only momentarily using our body as a vessel before its journey to the afterlife. The soul and the body, then, are connected, and this needs to be remembered.

> *Then the Lord God formed man of dust from the ground, and breathed into his nostrils the breath of life; and man became a living being.*
> (Genesis 2:7)

In defending, upkeeping, and saving our soul, we are in truth referring to that innermost part of ourselves which is the image of God. The body becomes a temple in lieu of the fact it is animated by the breath of God, housing the soul-as-image of God. Yet, in distinction to pre-Christian understandings of the spirit (largely Platonic), we are not to disregard the body (and by extension matter) entirely, as something not worth our time. No, for in the Christian understanding, the body too—as with all things—is God's creation, and will equally be risen up on the last day. So unlike pre-Christian understandings of the soul, whereby all that was deemed of importance was the spirit and the 'higher', Christianity holds body and soul as a unity, to be kept harmonious until the day of judgement.

With this divide, however, comes the negation of such questions as 'Where is the soul?' or 'What does the soul look like?' As it is something that is outside space and time (non-material), we cannot give it a form in common sense and thus we also cannot locate it spatially. Our connection with the soul, then, as with our connection and communion with all things divine, is outside of sensuality and found in that tranquil silence that needs to be allowed and *opened* to.

Though it is an emphatically quantified way of thinking about the soul, I like to think of it as an eternal record of deeds done during its union with the body here on earth. The body is mortal and the soul immortal, and yet the soul cannot act without the use of the body and its senses. As such, the soul has only the time of its body to meet the 'requirements' of salvation, to redeem itself. In a sense, the soul is that which is to be put before the Lord upon the day of judgement. Often it is metaphorically perceived as handing over two books, one of our good deeds and one of our bad (the latter usually much larger). Yet, in truth, that which shall be presented, that which *is* those two books, *is* our soul and thus ourselves. Our soul, as a record of our deeds, is that which stands before the Lord and—whether it wishes to or not—shall present all that it undertook whilst allowing its God-Willed life.

> *The unity of soul and body is so profound that one has to consider the soul to be the 'form' of the body: i.e. it is because of its spiritual soul that the body made of matter becomes a living, human body.*
>
> (*Catechism*, 1996, #365)

The soul is the first principle of any human being. If man is, then it is because the soul as God's breath was breathed into him. The soul as the form of the body is thus that which makes the thing what it is. Without a soul, there is no such thing as man.

As I have stated, however, the soul can be symbolically viewed as an indexer of one's deeds, a book of one's life presented before God in the afterlife. What, then, are our options after death, where are our deeds taking us?

The afterlife

One of the key questions for all undertakings in life is the 'why', as to why we're doing it altogether. Where are these actions going to take us? What is the end of all things? Being a Christian and *practising* Christianity is no different. This isn't to say, however, that the ends justify the means, only that the end of that which comes after life is often at the forefront of many Christian's minds. I am speaking of course of heaven, purgatory, and hell. These three names that have become so commonplace within our culture have come to respectively signify states even beyond their original theological meaning. Their appropriation within culture, however, rarely does them justice. More often than not heaven is viewed as a place full of clouds and harps, hell is fire, brimstone, and niche punishments, and purgatory rarely gets a look in. The problem with this form of aesthetically-focused appropriation is that it obscures the spiritual reality of the afterlife in favour of an approachable material one; material suffering is far easier to understand than spiritual suffering. I believe, practically speaking, that the three forms of the afterlife known to the Christian are best understood as states of being. In perceiving them this way, one can begin to see that state which is already present in their lives. Have they cast off the shackles of the world and seek always to follow a higher calling? Does one feel there is yet much to be purged for their life to make sense? Or does one feel entirely lost and disoriented, simply abiding by the whims of each passing moment? Let's look at the reality of the afterlife.

There's a single fact of life, unavoidable by *all*, and that is death. We *will all* die someday. Considering it's one of the few absolutes of life, it's peculiar that discussion of it is commonly avoided, and when it *is* mentioned it's in a negative light. Death is part of life and one day it will 'happen' to all of us. From the Christian point of view, this bears repeating and emphasising due to the fact the three destinations of the afterlife are unavoidable. The faith and fruits of our lives, imbued within our immortal souls, are those which grant us our reward or declare us to be punished. Each of our souls—as being immortal—is already within eternity, yet it cannot act of its own accord due to its inherent lack of sensuality (the five senses), a body, and reason. And so, the soul, as within a sensing body, has only the limited time of that material 'vessel' to beget a good and Christian life. Every man and woman's life is referred to Christ. Have we lived as Christ preached and have we united our death to His? Have we, given all the distractions and passions of the world, taken up our Cross and lived in accordance with a conscience whispered by God? If so, then entrance to heaven—either immediately or after some purification—shall be granted, or in our ignorance and rejection of the Lord, are we to be damned into hell? This all sounds rather limited, but hopefully, I will be able to explain why it must be so.

We begin, figuratively speaking, at the 'top', in heaven. We are told that *'The just shall go into life everlasting'* (Matthew 25:46). Those who arrive in heaven immediately after death, are those who died entirely free from sin, and therefore also all *punishment* due to sin (which I will get to when we come to purgatory and hell). Rarely, however, is there prolonged conversation on the actual 'what' of heaven. We may call something heavenly, or say 'I was in heaven' when looking back upon a certain event, but the specifics of the actual place are lost. Those who arrive in heaven are those who died in God's grace, with love for Christ in their hearts, accepting Him to the very end. As a reward, they are in a certain sense returned to the Eden yearned for all their life, finally receiving that which truly allows them to be content. For in heaven one finally sees God face to face, known as the 'beatific vision'. For here and now we only see a reflection of God within His creatures and His creation, in heaven we shall see Him directly, fully open to us and us to Him. Of course, how can I write of that which is not of this world?

That which I cannot—until death—have experience of? The Catechism and Scripture write of 'life, light, peace, paradise', and it is only clear that the rewards and contentment of heaven are beyond conception and that, in the words of Fr John Laux, 'the ills of life will be no more'. Ultimately, we understand that we shall reign with Christ, fulfilling God's Will eternally amidst heavenly glory. One fact of heaven that is often left aside in common appreciation of the heavenly Kingdom, is that the rewards of heaven are not in degree equal for all. *'Every man shall receive his own reward according to his own labour'* (1 Corinthians 3:8), and yet, amidst this inequality, all are content and happy.

Purgatory

The question we have to ask ourselves now is: What is it that momentarily or permanently stops one from entering heaven? What is it which hasn't been achieved or understood that forbids entry, therein causing further purgation (purgatory) or damnation (hell)? So, one's eventual destination is determined by their relationship with sin. If one is entirely free from sin—primarily in the case of Saints—then they go straight to heaven. But what of those who fully accept Christ, is full of God's grace, and yet didn't quite meet the mark with regards to purging themselves of all sin? Such people will find themselves heading to purgatory.

If we're to think about the relationship between the body and the soul once more, the soul is already in eternity due to its very nature and yet unable to act without a body, we will come to understand that the stage within which we have a living body (life), is, therefore, the only stage of our existence where we can 'pay the debt' of the sins we commit. Once our temporal, material body is dead, and the soul is detached, there is no longer any possibility of sense or movement and therefore no longer any possibility of *work*. And so, those faithful souls who die with *venial* sins remaining go to purgatory, a place wherein their remaining sins shall be purged. The answer is clear as to why those with remaining sin cannot enter heaven, for heaven by its very definition is a place of divine perfection, where God's fire burns pure as crystal, and if it were the case that any imperfection could enter into perfection, then it would no longer be so.

This leads to a discussion of just what it is about one's life and way of being which leads them to heaven, purgatory, or hell. What is the foundation which allows or disallows entry? It is one's acceptance of God and of God's Will. The extent to which one has faith in the Lord and trusts in His voice. If it is such that one gets to the end of their time on this earth, they hold Christ firmly in their hearts, and yet there are still a few little (venial) sins floating around which have gone unnoticed, perhaps due to ignorance, then such imperfections must be purged before one can enter heaven. Such souls can—once dead—do nothing about their punishment in purgatory, for they are only a soul and not a body. They shall be certain of their salvation, but it's a matter of experiencing the suffering purgation for the time being. A common question is 'What exactly *is* this suffering?' It's certainly an interesting question due to the fact that 'suffering', when removed from a solely material context, appears to become something different from what we regularly know.

This leads us to an overlooked factor regarding our understanding of all three afterlife destinations, they are all a certain 'fire'. And before we get to the famous 'fires of hell', we need to understand what this 'fire' is altogether. Hebrews 12:29 refers to God Himself as a *'consuming fire'*, and 1 Corinthians 3:11–15 states that each human shall be judged by a certain type of fire someday, a fire-related—for those of less purity—to suffering and purgation. Such *fire* needs to be viewed with regard to God's omnipresence—the presence of God is everywhere at the same time—therefore stating that God is in heaven, purgatory, and hell. If he wasn't in any of these places then he wouldn't be omnipresent. How can it be, then, that God is in a place considered Godless (hell), and a place of purgation and imperfection (purgatory)? Such omnipresence is clearly not related to spatiality or stereotypical talk of location. It's not that God is materially somewhere as the liquid fills a glass or an object takes up space in a room. No, here we are firmly speaking once more of the inner Kingdom—*'The Kingdom of God is within you'*. We are speaking of the fact God is omnipresent as the Creator of all things, and—most emphatically—the Creator of our souls, the part of us that is eternal and thus connected to the afterlife. It is *from* this omnipresence then that a personal relationship *with* God via our own free will is formed, thereby giving the appearance that the flames of heaven, purgatory, and hell are different, whereas they are in fact one and the same yet made different by individual differences of disposition.

How is it, then, that the same fire can cause such disparate conditions? God's fire can be nothing but goodness, love, and mercy. So how can it be that when showered with such love some are content, some are avoidant, and some find themselves in pain? To explain why this is

I shall turn to a relatively well-known allegory—The Allegory of the Long Spoons. Within this tale, it is said that heaven and hell are both the same identical banquet, set out along a very lengthy table, and all of those who are seated at this table have no elbows (or at least, their elbows cannot bend). Due to this (metaphorical) alteration of self, it is such that no one can feed themselves, and each is to feed the person opposite them (or feed others generally). In heaven, all who find themselves at this table are quite content, in hell all are miserable, and, in purgatory, one might say such people are working out what it means to feed others.

This allegory is a very short encapsulation of the difficulties of being a Christian, especially within the modern world. It's this difficulty, of existing and living as Christ simply told us to, which begets the difference in the quality of God's fire. For it is not that the fire changes, but our own internal ignorance, stubbornness, and blockages mutate it into a destination of our own selection. The most drastic change in this destination I will explain when I speak of hell, but for now, let us remain in purgatory.

If we think of this allegory in relation to purgatory, we may imagine someone seated at the table who perhaps wishes to feed some but not others, is annoyed at the selection of food or design of the table, or perhaps it is someone who believes in certain aspects of the display could have performed a better job. The point is that what is being purged is one's crystallised, individual will, as a means to allow an openness for God's Will which is right, just, and that which upholds all. Purgatory *does* hurt, it's the same fire as hell with regard to the pain with the important exception that one understands that the suffering is that which will allow them to eventually enter heaven and witness the beatific vision, an understanding which begets an openness and acceptance of God's Will. What happens, however, if one simply *doesn't* accept God, and refuses to accept God?

Hell

Now we finally get to hell. We make our way to the figurative gutter of all things. The home of the devil, The place—we have come to understand from popular media—of strange punishments tailored to one's niche sins, everlasting fire and agony, and of course the horned Prince of Darkness overseeing all. The majority of these statements—even though they may contain a pinch of truth—are misaligned in their focus and concentrate (rather ironically) on the emphatically worldly aspects of hell.

I still consider the single greatest quotation regarding the reality of hell to come from C.S. Lewis' *The Problem of Pain* (1940), in which he states that 'that the doors of hell are locked on the inside'. This short and sharp quip encapsulates everything I seek to expand upon from here. The notion of locking from the *inside* emphasises the reality of free will and thus of individual choice. As we shall see when we arrive at the section on faith, much of what it means to be a Christian isn't necessarily always gift or grace, but a matter of *choice* as to whether or not one accepts the gifts freely given them by God. As such, there can be no such thing as 'no choice', for to knowingly refuse is to ignore and deny God. The ascetic and hermit Richard Rolle often spoke of those who hadn't accepted Christ as 'the rejected'. Certainly a very powerful statement, perhaps utilised to bring them around to their folly. But to reverse this term, 'the rejected', and see that in truth such people reject themselves is to get closer to the truth. For how can one be *rejected* from infinite love and mercy *except* by their own hand? This leads me to the actual reality of hell.

The place of hell, in a single sentence, is *eternal separation from God*. Four words encapsulate the most thorough and unimaginable of eternal punishments. It is true that there are (possibly) the famous sensual pains of hell—burning pitch, rising flames, etc. But ultimately these are pale in comparison when seen against the *pain of loss* which is the true punishment of hell. Allow me to get a touch existential here as a way to articulate the unfathomable nature of this pain, this loss. For there appears to be, in all the years of human existence, not one recorded case of a human being entirely content in their existence, entirely harmonious or at home in life. One might argue that we call such people Saints or Enlightened, but it is the case that the peace of those figures is found via their relationship with something outside of themselves and outside of the world, and therein their peace and contentment shall come to a true fulfilment when they move from this world to the next; the most peaceful and calm of all human beings is only so because of their patience in the face of the *next* life, the *after*life. It can only be that it is He who upholds all things Who can be the spirit which fulfils all ills and strife, Who makes one's existence complete and brings the final peace. Without acceptance of He one merely exists in their current, worldly state of continual disorientation of drifting, never able to find knowledge or experience sufficient for an unquestionable pure peace. Imagine, then, if you will, such a case wherein not only does one bear minor witness to the peace which shall eventually make them whole, but they also *reject* that peace! This is hell.

The world, as the kingdom of Satan, seeks to lead us astray and trick us at every turn. It attempts to make the finite appear eternal and the eternal appear finite. It proclaims darkness the victor and makes a pretence out of all its minor victories, not once attending to the fact that the (false) battle of Good and Evil was 'won' when Christ sacrificed Himself on the Cross. Death, the devil, and Darkness were beaten via the Lord sacrificing Himself and His only Son on the Cross, and therefore everything else becomes but folly, a trick born out of pride and malice. Hell is to *deny* and *reject* He who died for our sins, who redeemed us, and who upholds all things and therein the completion of ourselves; to reject God is to reject pure Love, a completely nonsensical act born solely out of pride. Hell is the place where one eternally 'knows better' than God, the place where one will pretend to be their very own little god forever. Hell is thus chosen because one's pride, as such, disallows them from accepting God's Love and Grace. Hell is chosen for separation from He who alone can make us whole again. Never forgiven, never loved, never whole, never unified, harmonious, or complete; forever searching, forever lost, and forever without root, this is hell. To aimlessly drift amidst aimlessness. To yearn with all one's being for some sort of answer, *forever*, knowing that one has forever given up the possibility of *ever* receiving the answer. An eternal ontological itch forever intensifying and never scratched. Surely the pain of a flame is almost forgettable in the face of such heart-wrenching, existential, self-chosen misery?

* * *

Exercise 5

Before undertaking this exercise sit for a few minutes and calm your thoughts.

Compounding the knowledge you have gained from the previous exercises, over the course of three days take ten minutes per day and meditate on hell, purgatory, and heaven. Try not to fall into strictly aesthetic versions of these states, but focus on the theological and spiritual reality of each. Hell as a place of separation from God, Purgatory as a place of purgation, and heaven as a place where one is alongside God. Think also of what hell, purgatory, and heaven are like as possible states here on earth, and what it is that causes them.

Journal your findings.

* * *

PART 2

THE PATH OF THE CHRISTIAN

Grace

Now that I have spent some time dusting away the cobwebs of modernity, alongside overviewing the basics of Jesus' life and the teachings of Christianity, it's time to delve into more nuanced discussions of basic Christian themes such as love, grace, and poverty. I've entitled this section The Path of the Christian because even though the first section allowed very clear-cut ideas—such as the Sacraments—to be understood, absolutism is often very difficult to carry forward into life with all its complexity and context. As such, I feel the actual path of any Christian, the one we walk on a daily basis, is really to be understood from the position of themes, traits, and gifts. For as one cannot arm wrestle someone to God, equally one will not win them over with extensive discussion on theology or proofs, the way to touch the heart of another with the reality of God is to act as He would, with love, charity, peace, and those virtues that come with *being* a Christian.

What is grace?

It is tough to say where it all begins, one's relationship with God, that is. Where can we ever say a certain discussion begins or ends? What are the foundations that allow such dialogues to *be* in the first place?

Everything is so interconnected and delicate that any attempt to trace a root is likely to pull it out altogether; if anything can be said of one's connection to God it's that it is most emphatically *delicate*.

If there can be such roots to our spiritual life they are not those which sprout from beneath in a fit of selection, but are those which are gifted to us from above. I am speaking of grace. Many focus on the *supernatural* aspect of grace when hastily defining it as a 'supernatural gift', often overlooking the fact that it is *given*, as a gift from God. That which one needs to enter eternal salvation isn't earned, or bought, but humbly accepted. Without this ordained gift, redemption is impossible.

Why do I feel it is so important to emphasise the importance of the *gift* aspect of grace especially? Because it is contrary to all that we are taught is right and correct with the world. In the modern world, complete with its emphasis on materiality, all is grasped, worked for, proudly flaunted as that which by our own fleshy blood, sweat, and tears we have by rights earned for ourselves; gifts are often covertly given for the sake of bolstering status, or in the hope of receiving one in return. Society in general is confused by acts of pure charity. And yet, the foundation of all Christian belief and possibility begins with such a divine gift, itself free and undeserved. From the outset, we are taught to develop humility in relation to that which has been given to us without *expected* returns. By such grace, we are accepted into God's embrace and called to become His children. The fact it is *undeserved* leaves a bitter taste in our modern mouths. We might think to ourselves, 'Well, why is it *I* don't deserve it? Says who?' This relates back to Original Sin. We are fallen, sinful creatures, our individual sins are the very same ones that nailed Christ to the Cross, the very same ones He died for. In its status as an unconditional, undeserved, and freely given gift, grace acts as the supernatural reality *par excellence* which sets the Kingdom of Heaven apart from the kingdom of man, for in this act of giving is revealed God's *unconditional* love. All He wants is for us to return to Him, and grace can be understood as the divine foundation of this invitation. This leads me to the question as to whether we can ignore, or even reject grace.

To answer this I need to turn to the separate forms of grace as understood by the Catholic Church. Namely, *sanctifying* (also called *habitual*) and *actual*. Let us begin with sanctifying grace. For many, this will be the beginning of their Christian journey because it is likely they were Baptised shortly after their birth, and likewise received such a grace as part of their Baptism. For sanctifying grace *stays* in the soul, it is this grace which allows the soul to become holy and supernatural, thus opening it for possible entry into eternal salvation. If sanctifying grace is within your soul at death, then it is understood that you can live in heaven (possibly with some time in purgatory beforehand). If, however, one's soul is without such a grace then it is understood to be, spiritually speaking, dead. It is therein without possibility of dwelling with God and separated from Him forever.

If we think (metaphorically) of sanctifying grace as being internal, that which is within us and within our souls, then we can think of *actual* grace as external. It is that peculiar divine nudge many feel in often fleeting moments which causes them to seek God, often without being able to put their finger on what exactly happened. One might ask, if we have sanctifying grace, then of what importance are actual graces? Well, we've all likely heard the idea that 'God has a plan for us all', and of course He does. What actual graces are doing, in ways we'll never be able to truly understand, is nudging us (though sometimes it's more like being pulled by the collar) along the path He has set out before us, and all we need to do is *listen*. Practically speaking He may lead our conscience to repentance and thus Confession, He may lead us to a specific Mass, to a certain prayer book, or down a different road, and as long as we listen in obedience, our faith and relationship with God will be deepened.

Now to the seemingly scary question, can we deny such graces? The answer is simple, short, and similar in all cases, the answer is yes. In the case of sanctifying grace, we lose it by committing a mortal sin, obviously inclusive of disbelieving in God and not having faith in Him. It can, however, be quite easily restored by the Sacrament of Reconciliation—Confession—which is a grace in itself; it's grace all the way down. This brings me to denial of actual graces. Quite simply, if in those moments when the Lord is calling us to do certain things, say certain prayers, or attend certain masses, we ignore these calls, we would be ignoring actual grace. This is quite common it seems, because actual graces, and thus the path God has set out for us doesn't always match with our own selfish desires.

It is always to be emphasised that the love between ourselves and God, or oneself and God, is *reciprocal*, yet begins with His outstretched hand. We accept His gift of love and from then on the deeper our relationship becomes with Him, the deeper His relationship becomes with ourselves. Likewise, the more we learn about Him, the more we come to learn about ourselves, for it would be impossible for one to learn more about the Creator without learning about His creation.

Why is it so important?

Why have I chosen, then, to put this discussion on grace first in this latter section of the practical life of a Christian? For the simple fact that it is before all things. If we are to turn to the Bible, to Matthew 4:18–20:

> [18] *And Jesus walking by the sea of Galilee, saw two brethren, Simon who is called Peter, and Andrew his brother, casting a net into the sea (for they were fishers).*
> [19] *And he saith to them: Come ye after me, and I will make you to be fishers of men.*
> [20] *And they immediately left their nets, followed him.*

It's in this passage from the Gospels that we can see grace most clearly. For we can literally see the nudge as given from God directly, wherein Jesus says to them: *Come ye after me*, we see grace in action. Peter (Simon) and Andrew most definitely had a choice at this moment as to whether or not they would or would not follow Jesus, but it is clear from the passage that they must have actively *listened* to His call and thereby followed Him. None of this could have happened without grace.

The very same calls are being sent down to us in our lives. Unlike Peter and Andrew however, we don't have Jesus—God incarnate—before us in human form, yet we are still undertaking the very same act of faith by understanding, in our hearts, that the call is coming from He who is Right and Just. But we can also see here, in but two small, short lines, just how delicate grace is. In but a fleeting moment the future of the Church was held in the balance of two men who needed to make a decision based upon faith alone, and so it is with our own lives.

And so when we turn to the big questions which arise after we've accepted God: Where are we going? How do we get there? What do we do?—all are built atop the foundation of God's love and mercy, which is grace. These questions, then, which revolve around ourselves (Where are *we* going? What do *I* do?) are in fact, always, blossoming first and foremost from God.

Man does not hold up his own existence, God does. Man cannot cause himself to be holy, this is God's gift. At all times and in all paths, we are in truth making a single decision between our own will and the Will of God, and as it is His Will which upholds all of creation—as a gift—to lean against this for the sake of our own selfish desires, is to act in an ungrateful and sinful manner.

It's important in another more practical and emancipatory way which I've already touched upon, which I feel the need to expand upon in more detail. Grace is anathema to the modern world and to the world in general. It goes against everything the *world* teaches us to be 'correct' and 'obvious'. All the supposed (false) emancipations of the world lead us only to a different state of worldliness. One might feel free if they acquire a tonne of money and can acquire all the goods their heart desires; one might believe themselves set free if their political ideology was to take root and overhaul society; and one may consider themselves emancipated if one shed all the baggage of their ego, reaching an elusive state of enlightenment, able to become detached in some sense. Yet, in all these states of seeming emancipation, the end result is merely one in which the person in question remains within a world which is more to their liking, nothing, qualitatively speaking, has changed. How can we call anything emancipative if it simply leads us into yet another prison cell which happens to be more to our liking? In this case are we not just masking our own selfishness?

In this manner, drawing on the notion of grace as our foundation, we can begin to unravel the often secularly derided idea of 'being a slave to Christ'. Nothing sets off the alarm bells of selfish man's materially focused freedom than suggesting that one should be a slave to Christ. Yet there are only two perspectives regarding this slavery, ignorance or acceptance. But first, what exactly is slavery? To be a slave to someone or something is to be entirely dependent on it, a state wherein one's whole life is subject to their master's will. If we are to begin with ignorance then, with those who lack faith, push God away, or simply do not believe in Him. Such people may very well state that from such a position they don't have any type of transcendent master and thus cannot be a slave. But this is not the case, for in their ignorance they avoid the reality of death, constraining their understanding to the mere 70–80 years they have on this planet. But life abhors a vacuum, and these are not people running *freely* from whom to whom, but slaves of immanent, worldly things. They become not slaves to God but to worldly idols. In the words of David Foster Wallace:

> If you worship money and things then you will never have enough. Worship your own body and beauty and sexual allure and you will always feel ugly ... Worship power—you will feel weak and afraid, and you will need ever more power over others to keep the fear at bay. Worship your intellect, being seen as smart—you will end up feeling stupid ...
>
> (*This Is Water*, 2009)

These are the modern world's new gods, the things which appear to uphold our lives. Yet, they clearly do not uphold *life itself*, the very fabric of existence. It is because of these newfound gods I state that grace is anathema to the modern world, for these gods are not gifts, they are earned and revered from a position of rightful ownership. We need not thank anyone for such things because we earned them. But their supposed emancipative potential is limited solely to the world, one can never get enough of gods, but of God, of Christ, there is no such thing as enough because He already is in all things. Here, then, we move to acceptance.

When one accepts God into their heart and listens to His call to them—itself an act of grace—they are becoming His slave. But this slavery is often misconstrued as something negative due to both the general connotations surrounding the notion of slavery, and the modern obsession which perceives any limitation of one's existence in a negative light. This is different. As we come to accept God and all the Truth that the journey brings along with it, we come to understand that this is not a slavery born from fear, hatred, domination, or lust, but one built upon love. If we are to look back at the previous sections concerning the original state of the world. Of Eden, of walking side by side with God in the garden, with the harmony which was created for us to exist within, born solely from the love of the Holy Spirit, we can see that this is not slavery by way of chains, but the only emancipative slavery that exists, the one which allows us the ability to cast off all chains of the world and potentially once again enter into that harmonious state with God.

Nothing *in the* world can give us any real freedom. It is only He who is outside of the world, and outside of time who can do so. For it is not an optional slavery like money or power. God created the world and everything in existence purely out, and of, His love for us. At first, we abided by this slavery in a state of harmony, and then Eve said 'No'. to God, rebelling against freedom, and thus entering humanity into the state of Original Sin. Such a state of slavery isn't optional for God is He who upholds all creation, we are beholden to His love for us without option. Our choice is only between accepting His calls for us to return to this original state of love (via grace) or continuing to create our own gods and revere the things of the world, and in turn push against He who upholds everything.

So to return to the original idea, that grace is anathema to the modern world, we can now understand it is so because entering into, and accepting, this gift from God equally begins to draw us away from the false promises of the world. Slowly transforming us into human beings who are in the world but not *of* it. For in accepting grace, one accepts Truth and denies falsity, the world still stands but it is put in its right place, and that which is always tertiary to the Love of God, a tool only for the cultivation of our God-Willed path through life. Why, then, is grace so important? Because it allows us an entry into the *only* thing which can ever fulfil us, ever allow us any semblance of truth, beauty, and contentment. Without grace we are merely pushing against life itself, wallowing around in our own dirt, trying to figure out answers to questions of our spontaneous creation; without grace, we enter into a life bereft of God, an eternally recursive state of confusion. In other words, we practically enter hell. But I will save talk of that for later.

What is it to have grace?

One may ask, then, what does it *feel* like to have grace? The short answer is that it differs from person to person. Some feel nothing at all, some feel at peace, many say they feel at home, and a few may even feel a sort of lightness. There is, however, no promise of anything when one receives grace. Grace being a supernatural gift means that it is not a materially tangible thing. It is not something we can pick up, show off to other people, or measure. It is of the divine; it is from God.

There is, however, one way to put grace in perspective, by looking at its negative. Theologically speaking the negative of being in the state of grace is being in the state of mortal sin. This state of sin is one in which we have gravely offended God, acted in such a way as to disobey His commandments, or wilfully refused to listen to His voice. So in a rough manner, the opposite of the *gift* of grace is our *selfish* acts within the world. The former is given, undeserved, and pure love, whereas the latter is grasping, 'rightfully earned', and undertaken from a place of greed.

To begin to practically understand the feeling of grace then, we can begin by articulating the feeling of its opposite, of our continual clutching at the world. Throughout life, we often find ourselves in a perpetual state of stress, of seeking some elusive thing that will be the final purchase or acquisition which at last quenches the strange emptiness we feel within ourselves. We jump from awards, to properties, to holidays, to bars, to cars, to events, and to countless books, all in the hope that the next *thing* will be the one that fulfils us. We find, though often from a point of ignorance, that this isn't the case. Even if we are not as satisfied as we at first thought we'd be, we tell ourselves it's because we overlooked some-or-other factor, and in truth it will be the *next* thing that will scratch our internal itch and the next, and the next, and then … you get the picture. The opposite of grace—which is mercy and love—is not the exact opposite of vengeance and hatred, but a state of confusion, of being lost. It is a feeling of knowing one needs a certain thing, but not knowing what that thing is or where it can be found. For if one hasn't the Grace of God, that doesn't necessarily mean they are hated by something else. It does mean that they are a creature who could be saved without possibility of salvation; a yearning in their heart for a home they know not of.

Grace gives one their eternal home, without which we feel stranded; without grace one runs from nothing to nothing, forever in the hope of something from below which shall never arise. And so even if it is that grace feels as nothing in a material sense, in the manner of heart and soul one will experience a satiation for a hunger they never knew they had. The gifts of the world are received in expectation, we await them with a palpable suspense, unwrapping them with glee. The gift of grace is given at the moment of acceptance, it is there from the moment we say with our heart 'Yes'.

To have grace is to walk with the will of the Lord, to walk His path amidst all Sacraments. In all phases of life to accept grace is to accept the Lord as He who gives the love, mercy, and beauty which is to be found within our lives. At first, we accept the eternal, sanctifying grace of Baptism, our entry into His Kingdom. Week by week one receives the grace and divine food of the Eucharist. Once a month one receives the grace of absolution and renewal via Confession (if they so choose). At the ultimate moment of joyous love between a man and woman, the couple receives the grace of marriage, to know that He is with them throughout. And finally, in our final hours, we receive the anointing of the sick, the grace of strength and courage amidst the end.

The relationship between grace and faith is reciprocal, one begets the other. Yet, this mutual love between man and God cannot first begin without us approaching the Lord's outstretched hand and accepting His gift:

> *⁸ For by grace you are saved through faith, and that not of yourselves, for it is the gift of God;*
> *⁹ Not of works, that no man may glory.*
>
> (Ephesian 2:8–9)

And no man may glory, for as grace is prior to faith it is not a gift of which we can boast. Grace simply *is*, the choice is ours whether we step towards it in a leap of faith. Grace is not a divine addition to reality, it is to accept He who upholds reality in its entirety. To accept it is to begin the subtle detachment from the world, from all the promises which can never be kept. It is to place one's foot on the narrow path with the faith that, in time, it shall deliver one Higher.

* * *

Exercise 6

It's time for another prayer. This time with a single purpose, to try to place oneself in a selfless position. It might be to ask for help, to ask for grace, or to ask for faith, the purpose being to see oneself as part of a far larger picture. One could choose their own words for this, and simply kneel and talk to God about their faults and the help they feel they need. Or, one could say what is commonly known as the *Peace Prayer* or the *Prayer of St Francis* (though it appears in none of his writings).

> *Lord, make me an instrument of your peace.*
> *Where there is hatred, let me bring love.*
> *Where there is offence, let me bring pardon.*
> *Where there is discord, let me bring union.*

> *Where there is error, let me bring truth.*
> *Where there is doubt, let me bring faith.*
> *Where there is despair, let me bring hope.*
> *Where there is darkness, let me bring your light.*
> *Where there is sadness, let me bring joy.*
> *O Master, let me not seek as much*
> *to be consoled as to console,*
> *to be understood as to understand,*
> *to be loved as to love,*
> *for it is in giving that one receives,*
> *it is in self-forgetting that one finds,*
> *it is in pardoning that one is pardoned,*
> *it is in dying that one is raised to eternal life.*

After one has said their prayer, sit in silence for five minutes and simply open yourself to God's grace.

Love

What is love?

From grace, we can move aptly into love, for grace itself is simply God's love. In much the same way that a vacuum of worship is not possible—we all worship *something*—so too is a vacuum of love impossible. Even those who we may proclaim to be heartless and full of hate are likely in love with something we cannot see, be it their egos or their possessions. For all people there are those things which they will happily give themselves over without thought for anything else; love can extend outwards in acts of kindness or charity, or it can protrude inwards in defence of ego or greed.

But the question still stands, what exactly *is* love? And not just love in general, but more importantly, what is God's love? In its vague assertiveness, this question and the statement 'God is love' consistently appear to baffle both atheists and Christians, despite the fact it's often the go-to statement regarding the reality of God. But like many seemingly obvious and overlooked remarks regarding Christianity and the divine, it's more often the case that we simply haven't sat down to think about what this means, or what exactly love even is.

I could lean on a definition at this point and state that love in general is *an intense feeling of deep affection*, but anyone who has been in love with another person would understand that this doesn't really hit the mark, largely because love is a *feeling* and its definition is *language*, and one cannot describe the other. This very same problem applies to the majority of definitions, and most emphatically applies to all language that relates to God, be it His love, faith, grace, kindness, and/or charity, no single word can suffice in describing the feeling one is imbued within their connection with the Lord. Let us begin with Scripture:

> *So we have come to know and to believe the love that God has for us. God is love, and whoever abides in love abides in God, and God abides in him.*
> (1 John 4:16)

When our love is forthwith *for* God, in the understanding that it comes from Him and *is* Him, therein love abounds. For in the sense that God is perfect and we have come into existence, the very fact we are alive is a decision made from the position of He who is perfect in all ways, and as such it is from His love that we are brought to life. Love is that state in which one would do *anything* for the loved in question, because of the pure fact of the love itself. It is that overwhelming, yet patient state of being which asserts what is right and what is meant to be without ever dominating reality; love is quiet, meek, kind, patient, tough, slow, and humble all at once, without ever being seen.

As with grace, love first comes from God for the very fact God *is* love. God and all His works are manifestations of His love; Creation, Incarnation, Resurrection, the Second Coming, these all are—or shall be—love, and performed from a position of love. From the position of He that upholds all things by His Will alone, and therein it follows that all are held up by God's love alone. In beginning from such a place, we can begin to format some definition of love by stating that it is clearly, at first, divine. Or in the case of man, the state of love—or giving love—springs forth from the divine source of grace.

When we love someone, or a community, or our family, the foremost difference between them and all other things is that we *remember* them. What one loves is often revealed in a crisis by way of them bringing to the fore that which they're most worried about. This notion of remembrance is where we can most clearly see God's love for us throughout history. As we've seen, humanity is *fallen*, we said 'No'. to God's Will (and therefore His love) and were cast out from the state of perfect harmony we once lived in (Eden). Of the many catastrophes of our history, of all the times we've disagreed with God, pushed against Him, and tried to have our own way, this was the worst.

At this juncture in our history, God could have forgotten about us, and left us to our fate of final death and toil, without any hope for redemption and salvation. But He didn't, He remembered us, and in (our) time, sent His one and only Son, Jesus Christ, to the world to die and suffer for all our sins upon the Cross. And as is said in Galatians 5:22–23: '*The fruit of the Spirit is love, joy, peace, patience, kindness, generosity, faithfulness, gentleness, and self-control*', so too are all such traits—springing forth first from the well of love—found within such acts of remembrance. For, from our perspective, in remembering us God continues the perfection that is His Will; simply within our existence and being we are remembered by God and thus loved by Him as creatures capable of the path of salvation.

What love isn't

How can we learn to love?

So now we understand what love both is and isn't, and equally what God's love (and grace) is and isn't, we find ourselves in a better position to begin enacting love, to begin bringing love into the world. Yet, as we've seen in relation to what has already been written, love—in alignment with grace—isn't necessarily something that can be commanded or controlled, as much as it is something that is to be allowed or accepted, and therein communed outwards via such grace. This all sounds a little abstract (once again), so let me try to turn things practical once more.

Love, in any practical, human sense, is always attempting to imitate the pure love which comes to us from God. This form of love coming to us from the Lord is unconditional, there are *no* conditions which we must meet for God to love us; *He loves us*, and the choice is simply whether we turn towards and accept this love. But His love didn't come for free, for we are fallen creatures who were in need of redemption. And so He sent His only son, our Lord Jesus Christ down to earth to suffer for the sake of our redemption. So pure is His love, His mercy, and His forgiveness, that He offered up His only Son as a path for us to return from our self-willed abandon. In thinking, then, of God's love and its reality of being unconditional, so too can we begin to form an understanding of the true meaning of what it is to love one another, love a community, love a person, love our children, or love generally.

We can see that more often than not love comes at a cost, it comes with some sort of sacrifice. Never anything as theologically major as the Passion, but still contextually a sacrifice within our own lives. Yet viewed from the light of God such sacrifice can be seen only as positive. We can see this in our own lives when we're imitating God and Christ, and what it is to truly love. For to marry out of love is to sacrifice much for one's partner and children, to love a community is to build it out of thought only for the community itself, and in general, to love something with the understanding of the pure Love of God, is to love it for the sake of that love alone, to love it simply because it is, and in being at all, it is *of God* and thus deserving of love.

Thus far this is still quite abstract, as it appears as if love keeps rotating into itself and becoming tautological. This is because this is the truth. Unconditional love, by its very nature as being unconditional, can never have any such thing as justification, for to justify it, would be to state that there is such a case wherein it would be undeserving of love. If we are even to begin to think of that which we seek to love as undeserving of love if it does X, Y, and/or Z, then we never loved it as purely as we could, and sought always to retain some sense of control with respect to our own beliefs about how the thing in question *should* be.

To say how someone, some group, or something *should* be is to project one's own 'correct' vision of the future, of beauty, and of justice onto the thing in question. It's to be so egoistic as to assume that one's own view is obviously correct for the simple fact that it is theirs. Often—but not always—such controlling behaviour subverts the purity of love to such a degree that one puts oneself in the position of God, attempting to form the future to their will as opposed to accepting the Lord's.

If such an understanding of love appears to you to be tough, to be hard work, or to be overly demanding, this is because pure love *is* all these things. For this we need turn no further than one of the more well-known passages of the New Testament, Peter's denial of Jesus in Luke 22:54–62:

> [54] *And apprehending him, they led him to the high priest's house. But Peter followed afar off.*
>
> [55] *And when they had kindled a fire in the midst of the hall, and were sitting about it, Peter was in the midst of them.*

[56] *Whom when a certain servant maid had seen sitting at the light, and had earnestly beheld him, she said: This man also was with him.*

[57] *But he denied him, saying: Woman, I know him not.*

[58] *And after a little while, another seeing him, said: Thou also art one of them. But Peter said: O man, I am not.*

[59] *And after the space, as it were of one hour, another certain man affirmed, saying: Of a truth, this man was also with him; for he is also a Galilean.*

[60] *And Peter said: Man, I know not what thou sayest. And immediately, as he was yet speaking, the cock crew.*

[61] *And the Lord turning looked on Peter. And Peter remembered the word of the Lord, as he had said: Before the cock crow, thou shalt deny me thrice.*

[62] *And Peter going out, wept bitterly.*

Before us, then, we have Saint Peter the Apostle, the Rock unto which the Church was to be built, the first Pope, and one of Christ's closest Apostles and friends, the man to whom Christ trusted everything. And yet what do we see him do at the time of his Lord's greatest misery, peril, and despair? We see him deny and betray Christ. And so, in front of the Lord—who has trusted all to Peter—he denies Him three times, and yet does Christ appear to ever hold anything against Peter? Does he even reprimand Him? Not at all. In the Gospel of John, we understand that as a balance for his triple denial of Christ, Peter affirms his love for Christ three times and restores the harmony. In this re-affirmation of Peter's love for the Lord, we aren't witness to some sort of bartering, but to a simple acceptance. For Christ was not angry, frustrated, or hostile to Peter, but simply waited for His love to be accepted, without condition for its giving.

And so we often feel or believe ourselves to be giving, kind, and ultimately loving people. But in our imitation of the pure Love of God, which has now been undertaken between the Lord and a man (Peter), we can begin to see how to possibly enact it, and just how far we likely fall away from this perfection. How often do we 'love' only out of some deeply secretive belief in compensation? Which communities do we love out of bolstering status or monetary gain? Which friends do we love only when the convenience to do so presents itself? Who and what, we should ask ourselves, are we willing to be entirely purged for? For only in acceptance of the complete loss of self can we say we truly, purely, love another as God loves.

To love in this pure sense might appear as an immense fear of emotion and giving, this is because it quite simply *is* immense. In fact, it's so immensely difficult that only God can do so infinitely and indefinitely. Any imitation of such love is just that, imitation, an attempt. But we must not think to ourselves that because any such attempt will never match with the purity of the Lord that our love is in vain. For we are fallen creatures, full of mistakes, errors, and fallibility. As it is famously quipped, 'To err is human'. And, in much the same manner, I do not think it controversial to state that *sin is human*. This is not to say that sinning and error are just to be accepted as part and parcel of existence and thus ignored, but that sin *is* to be accepted as part of one's journey as a fallen being. And, in returning to love, by pushing ourselves to see and understand that which *we* put in the way of our imitations of God's love, we can begin to see what needs to be purged as a means to get closer to God.

To reiterate this point and to equally emphasise the purity of God's love we can think of those people and things we love. We can, if we are honest with ourselves, begin to draw out those conditions which might make such love impossible. Perhaps if there were certain frustrating individuals within a certain group we would simply give up; if our neighbour said the wrong thing we begin to dislike them; if our loved one became disfigured it might be that we would move on; it may even be that if our children committed certain acts we would disown them. Such events seem extreme and yet are common occurrences throughout many people's lives. Lifetimes filled to the brim with known and unknown conditions, and therein love which dissipates often at the meagrest sign of personal disagreement. Our love is often fickle, despite all our attempts to tell ourselves otherwise.

Whereas God, in His perfection, can never be fickle. He does not hold grudges. He does not act out of some arbitrary sense of fairness or equality which changes from season to season. His love is acted out for the sake of love alone, without condition, as a grace. He loves you because you are His creation, and He created you for the purpose of you loving Him and He loving you. You were born to love and be loved, and in this, He shall never forget you, and we must strive to never forget Him.

* * *

Exercise 7

Before undertaking this exercise sit for a few minutes and calm your thoughts.

Open with a short internal prayer using your own words, possibly asking for the Lord to guide you, or simply continuing a conversation you've already been having with Him. Once that is done, discursively meditate on love. *Discursive meditation* is simply reflexive meditation that concentrates on a single theme, piece of writing, or even a single word over the course of the meditation. In this instance, one can either choose to meditate on the idea of love or on the feeling of love. Sit for 10–15 minutes and try as hard as you can to hold the idea of love in your thoughts, allow it to open and grow, but all the while keep it within the bounds of 'love'.

Journal your findings.

If you wish to extend this exercise, for the next week take a separate theme for each day—grace, hope, faith, God, being, etc.—and perform the meditation the same as above. If you find a certain theme has a lot more to say to you than the others, perform multiple meditations on the same theme over separate days. (Little and often is better.)

* * *

Faith

What is it?

Now that we have grace and love, the somewhat interchangeable and given foundation of all things, we can begin to turn the direction of this book a little more toward ourselves. However, this new direction, which is focused more on man isn't necessarily narcissistic, is a discussion that begins the question as to what it is we are to *do*. For we now have the history, the Sacraments, and a basic understanding, alongside a base and possible openness to love and grace, and it is from this position we can ask how it is we are to act and as such begin our actual journey of *faith*.

Faith, second to love, is a word often carelessly thrown around without thought for its fragility. 'Have faith!' we may proclaim amidst the most fickle of endeavours. But what can we truly say of a 'faith' which has as its foundation a collection of material evidence that allows us to proceed with ease? It cannot be the case that we can call any such worldly faith, born after calculation, as anything other than an inside bet. No, here I am writing about faith in the divine, faith in God. That which the Catechism defines as 'a personal adherence of man to God'. can then be (in part) understood as an adherence between he who knows not and is unsure and He Who Is and is Truth entirely. An adherence between creation and its Creator. A unilateral relationship between the Above and the below, with one side finding its communication and connection born from uncertainty, intuition, conscience, and hope.

Put plainly, faith is a personal or communal relationship with God. It is a grace. For from grace itself, the grace of the love that upholds us, it follows that such grace comes forth that gives us ears to hear and eyes to see. To *have faith* is to open oneself to the grace of the Word, it is to retain that which one has been granted, the gentle communication of God which balances itself between all moments; to be given, to accept, to keep.

There are many misconceptions attributed to the idea of faith, many being born from vague collective agreement of what it is to 'be faithful'. To have faith, we commonly hear, is possible to be overly emotional, often loud and proud, to have a certainty bordering on condescension. But all such proclamations once more arrive from a place far away from the delicate nature of the Lord. All these opinions erase the reality of the interplay between faith and choice, between belief and free will.

After all the dust had—and has—settled, after Eden, the Fall, the Passion, and the Resurrection—after the narrative that makes the connection between man and the Lord what it is and what it can be—a single element remains for man which settles all that he will or will not be, that element *is* choice itself, the free will of all men. And so as we receive grace as given outside of our own doing and in such a moment feel, intuit, or in small part understand the Love of God, so too do we have the *decision* to have faith in such feelings, thoughts, and gestures. Within the act of grace God's love is revealed to you, it is your choice to have faith in that which has been granted to you, regardless of any specific feelings.

It is a lesson to take forward and one of the hardest to learn individually, that is, that faith isn't always correlated with any specific feeling and rarely adheres to the common notion of experiencing elation or even a subtle internal elevation. Faith, like God, is often peculiar in its ways. One might hear the Word of God and note a sense of hesitancy, disagreement, or even internal contradiction, but beneath all which is usually hastily piled atop this act of hearing and obeying from our personality is the deep (or should I say high) understanding that the Word is the Truth. Rarely, if ever, does our openness and acceptance of God's Word fall into direct agreement with our own desires and wishes. In fact, faith, as a choice—and thus a form of test—can usually be understood as such if there *is* some form of push-and-pull, some felt the tension, and some understood the notion that to open in either agreement or disagreement would be to pass onto a right or wrong path, and thus to enter into—so to speak—new life.

With faith, therefore, is entry and retention of the narrow way:

> *[13] Enter ye in at the narrow gate: for wide is the gate, and broad is the way that leadeth to destruction, and many there are who go in thereat.*
> *[14] How narrow is the gate, and straight is the way that leadeth to life: and few there are that find it!*
> (Matthew 7:13–14)

As we continually make the choice to accept the voice of the Lord which we are given as a grace, we too retain our adherence to the narrow way.

Faith is a choice

Faith is a gift. One which is found hand-in-hand with grace. The fact of faith being a grace tends to occlude the reality of human agency regarding faith as an action, as a choice. It will appear strange that something which is given freely and without condition by God is equally something we have the choice to accept or ignore. Yet, if we are to look back at the brief history of Christianity given at the beginning of this book, one will see that after all things it is, for man, only the decision itself that remains. Is one going to choose God or power? God or status? God or self? God or, ultimately, nothing? Christianity makes no sense without free will. None of that which I have and plan to speak about here—grace, faith, love, goodness—can *be* without a choice on behalf of the received to accept and undertake with their own agency.

Grace is a gift freely given that allows us to know God, to—abstractly—enter into communication with Him, and one can always refuse to communicate or turn down a gift. Love can never be anything other than a choice, forced love is absolutely paradoxical and meaningless. An act of goodness undertaken not from the heart but from etiquette or compulsion may be externally moral, yet internally it lacks any root. And so too can faith, if it is to mean what it means, only be a choice willingly taken.

As the Catechism states (almost immediately, thus emphasising that nothing more can follow if this *decision* isn't made):

> *We begin our profession of faith by saying: I believe or We believe. Before expounding the Church's faith, as confessed in the Creed, celebrated in the liturgy, and lived in observance of God's commandments and in prayer, we must first ask what 'to believe' means. Faith is man's response to God, who reveals himself and gives himself to man, at the same time bringing man a superabundant light as he searches for the ultimate meaning of his life.*
> (Catechism, 1996, #26)

This profession of faith, this beginning of liturgy and worship begins with the covertly simple statement *I believe*. Within these two words is folded such a multifaceted declaration of the heart, one is astounded at how their simplicity suffices. For in stating our belief, our faith—in declaring our decision—we are attending to an eternal desire many reject in lieu of the world. A desire 'written in the human heart'. The choice of faith—the choice to *have* faith—may very well be the *only* choice we, as humans, actually have. For it is from this choice that the oft-declared 'emptiness' we find within ourselves throughout daily life is healed. Faith is the only answer to the repetitive, existential search for 'something more'. And it is not the case that as we declare *I believe* or *we believe* that one is lifted from their seat on a cloud of light, nor is it that there is any definitive feeling to speak of, for faith as a choice is an acceptance of what already is and what has been all along, which is to say God's voice written upon your soul and speaking to you as you are.

Of course, one cannot make this choice of faith blindly, clinging to it solely because they wish it were true. And much to the dismay of many 'new atheists', it's incredibly difficult for someone to believe something they deep down know to be untrue, especially if such a belief makes their life more difficult than it need be were the reality different, as is true with Christianity (to paraphrase C.S. Lewis—being a Christian is hard work). The point is that faith doesn't make something real. One could have faith that they'll float off a cliff, but soon find evidence to the contrary when they walk off. This book, however, isn't an apologetic, but an introduction, so I won't so much as defend the justification of faith (which is needed), but attempt to make apparent here how that justification may manifest itself, thereby articulating how it is that faith is.

All have been set free—once more—Christianity falls apart if there is no free will. As one traverses life, with all its trials and tribulations, ups and downs, one finds—as I have already stated, and as I imagine many who are reading this understand—that there is little to nothing that fulfils us, that makes us content. Ask any person at random what they desire in life and the answer is likely to be happiness, contentment, and peace (or some variant/synthesis of these things), humans wish to feel settled or 'at home'. And yet, the very fact we ask such questions regarding the meaning of life and give such answers (which are yet to be found) makes it apparent that such desires are rarely fulfilled within our current way of existence. It is the case because the search for meaning has been entirely contained to the material world (to things and stuff), whereas, reality is far larger than the material world, and so we allow ourselves to be ignorant of those other factors such as God. And this is where the justification of faith begins, this is where the choice becomes more than just a choice and enters into experience. One, both metaphorically and literally (Baptism), tests the waters. Arriving at the end of materiality and all the unspoken promises of the modern world, one finds themselves contemplating the quiet voice in their heart which has struck them under many other names (conscience being a common one). We may not know what this 'feeling' is, we may not know what to do with it, or how to 'use' it, but it's most definitely real.

Herein is where one takes the famous *leap of faith*. Abiding by something which is not solely reason, thought, or emotion, one gives oneself over to a choice that is beyond choice. But this decision can truly never be blind, for it is not the case that it is irreversible, and if such a leap is found to be false one can return just as quickly. And yet, most don't return. Most find something on the other side of this leap which begins a long process of healing, something (in Truth Some*one*) which is qualitatively beyond anything which made an attempt at contentment before. And of course, this leap is different from what was waiting after his leap already and always *was*. You were always loved, you were always thought of, and you were always forgiven, it is only that in denying yourself the choice to have faith, you in turn denied yourself connection to God, and in doing so became ignorant of He that made you and the soul of the very self you are; God is He that created us as His creation out of love, in remaining ignorant of Him we remain ignorant of ourselves.

How do we grow it?

Now we understand what faith is, and, in part, how we acquire it, a practical question one might ask themselves is 'Well, okay, but how exactly do I grow faith?' This is a peculiar question because faith is unlike that which is brought about *solely* by reason, it is in a certain sense *beyond* reason, and in asking a question regarding the acquisition of something beyond we mistakenly conflate quantity and quality. For it is not so that a certain person, by way of some-or-other virtue or merit, has X amount of faith and another person has Y, no one but God can look truly into the heart of another and understand the sincerity and depth of their faith, and so questions of how much or how often, questions relating to a 'tallying-up', these are inquiries already thwart with error.

In a strange sense, *we* cannot 'grow' our faith in any manner akin to the usual sense something is grown. For instance, one grows a plant via a reasoned understanding that certain amounts of water, soil, and sunlight in correct proportions will beget a better, healthier state of growth, perhaps even a terminal growth beyond which nothing more is possible. Yet in this example, it is clear that it is *we* who control when the plant is watered, what soil it will be planted into, and where it will be placed with respect to sunlight. Our acts of kindness towards the plant are gifts that are entirely outside of its control. This relationship is mirrored in man's faithful relationship with God. Man's faith is not his own but only ever His.

In the words of John Henry Newman:

> … the arguments for religion do not compel anyone to believe, just as arguments for good conduct do not compel anyone to obey. Obedience is the consequence of willing to obey, and faith is the consequence of willing to believe.
> (*Discourses to Mixed Congregations*, 2022, p. 224).

And so we can see that despite all modern proclamations to the contrary human reason has quick and clear limitations. In spite of its supposed clarity, rigour, and exactness, reason can only ever be a sibling within a much larger family, full as they commonly are with love, dysfunction, argument, agreement, and authority. Reason alone—especially within modernity—acts in a panic, anxious to quickly curtail all those lucid and authentic parts of human experience which cannot be made to swiftly succumb to materiality and empiricism. Ruling solely from its own kingdom alone, it hasn't time for emotion, intuition, assent, conviction, grace, and faith, even though such experiences make up a large part of human experience. When acting within the confines of its own rationale, reason is a mercenary of worldly control, hegemonically belittling and overpowering that which is beyond it. As such, in asking the question as to the 'acquisition' of faith, we ask a question that can never be answered with reason alone. Do not misunderstand me, for reason plays a role up to a point, but it is the decision that is to be made upon the limitrophe of reason which opens one to God and God to one; it is a decision that has already been made and we need only open and accept, for faith is a gift eternally and infinitely given, a Hand outstretched forever that we need only humble ourselves towards.

It is this metaphor I will expand upon to try to open up this discussion on *increasing* one's faith. Faith is grace, and faith is a gift from God. This gift, then, as we will now understand is given freely and unconditionally. And so, as simply as one can put it—faith is. One can imagine the outstretched Hand of God as simply *being*. For that which is offered as a gift (grace and faith), in being unconditional and freely given, simply is. We could imagine a corridor at the 'end' of which is God's gift to man, his faith. All a man needs to do is ... walk down the corridor. The gift *is* there, it—once again—simply is. Yet one will find that such a walk isn't so easy, and as they begin their journey towards this love and light, things begin to appear in the corridor which blocks out the light. They may even find—especially as they enter adulthood—that they even begin to drag things into the corridor and then become befuddled as to why they can no longer receive God's gift. In time many might find their own personal corridors so full to the brim with stuff that is beyond appears to have disappeared altogether. But of course, it could never be said that a gift freely given without condition of acceptance could *ever* disappear, it can only be the case that one has blocked it from view in an act of ignorance. Time goes by and one ages a little more and finds that all the stuff in the corridor has amounted to nothing, and they look and look at it trying to figure out what they must have missed. They have missed nothing, for one comes to realise that it can never be an act of material or worldly acquisition that fulfils us for that which is truly *us*—our soul—is not of this world and is already beyond and within the eternal, and as such, it can only be that which is also beyond which can lead to fulfilment.

When we look once again at our own corridors, our own paths between us and God, we can now see that the gift given to us is *there*, it is. Any sense unto which we can increase or grow faith is largely a matter not of acquisition or of more faith, but an act of revealing the gift which was and *is* there all along. One does not increase faith but reveal its perfect fullness; one does not *gain* more faith but humbles themselves to be more open; one does not grasp faith, one accepts it; one does not *take* faith and possess it, one seeks to understand the spiritual poverty of their own corridor to God and in doing so, in meekness, allow faith as unconditioned to be as it was all along.

The difference and mystery of that which grows and yet *already is*, how can this be? Here we need only turn to the short parable of the mustard seed from Matthew 13:31–32 to reveal this paradox:

> [31] *Another parable he proposed unto them, saying: The kingdom of heaven is like a grain of mustard seed, which a man took and sowed in his field.*
> [32] *Which is the least indeed of all seeds; but when it is grown up, it is greater than all herbs, and becometh a tree, so that the birds of the air come, and dwell in the branches thereof.*

That smallest of seeds, almost indiscernible to the eye grew into a crop of life and sustenance. Let us then think of seed, nut, and root. For if one was ignorant of life, innocent and naive to its functions, all acts of growth could not be. If attending to the world as a child one found before themselves an acorn and a full-grown oak tree, surely one would consider the man insane who declared that one arose from the other. How could it be that the mightiest of all trees, that pure symbol of strength and stability, found its beginnings in life contained within a tiny acorn? But as it is with the nut and tree, so too with faith. Everything needed for faith to become *what it already is* is itself founded within what is already there. Acorns and seeds do not doubt their nature, I have yet to meet such a nut that questions its possibility of becoming what it all along was meant to be. It is man alone who proudly doubts his ability to follow innate, God-given nature. And what is it men and women do instead exactly? They squander and question, stumble around making excuse after excuse, justifying to themselves why it is preferable to remain within that infantile hard shell they so protect. And is there anything sadder, if not more pointless than an acorn that never manages to find soil or ground from which to grow? A seed denied its nature is only an empty vessel waiting to degrade and drift silently into time.

The oak and crop, neither groaned of their growth up towards the sun; nor do we hear regret from nature and life itself for the circumstances of its fate, whether it was full of vibrancy or found within the shade. No, the mustard seed knows only of its inherent nature and, in a simple matter of *complete acceptance*, opens to it ... whatever the weather. Man declares himself different! Taught or justified, we pronounce that something is always in the way, that the sun needs to move for us, that the soil could be better, and that others need to water our lives more often. And if not we shall moan and whine and whinge like lukewarm domesticated daffodils who fold the moment their owners leave for the holidays! And yet as nature is, so too is man, for each of us holds within ourselves such a seed of faith, be it from the context of an oak growing amidst wide plains, a sunflower tucked in a suburban garden, or a weed courageously striking up from between some paving. Faith, the growth that already is. But we do so indulge in getting in our own way.

So it is that no discussion on faith can be complete without the dark mirror of doubt. Such a situation, wherein the imperfection is founded within the possibility of perfection, is the enclosed fate of man. No one dares ask why the snake was in the Garden of Eden in the first place, already known as that subtle, sly beast. But it is the snake as the agent of possible imperfection who opens the way to perfection; *a smooth sea never made a skilled sailor*, says Roosevelt, so too does tranquil weather not make a robust oak. Do these symbols of growth of which I have been speaking themselves yield to external factors? Or is it only ever that they grow until the last? But once more, what of man! That foolishly proud being who upon stubbing their toe denounces a lifetime's effort! And yet we mustn't be so hard on ourselves, for we are not so smart, and never shall be. We declare ourselves to know and know not, we state with our emotions and pretend it is intelligence, and we believe we know better than our God-given selves. One needs to watch masses of men and women scamper to and fro amidst cities and understand that in truth all they are witnessing are seeds attempting to grow themselves, rather than allowing themselves to grow. The difference is subtle yet important. The doubts arise and we may seek tricks and reason, rationale, and habit, avoiding the clear fact that doubt itself proves the fact of belief. Doubt is found in the silly seed which seeks to sever its own roots in hopes of a better future. But there, in that strange, stretching abyss that claws at our heart as doubt departs us from faith is the feeling itself of doubt's own destruction. Doubt is the tyrannical emptiness that interjects uncertainty without once presenting an alternative;

doubt begets its own doubt, and one is then lost in a loop of nothingness, clinging as they go to all kinds of other little nothings such as possessions or status. Faith is firm as it is, wherever it is. Faith is a completeness forever opening and growing.

One may find faith anywhere, amidst the best of life's fruits and the worst of its strife, for it is already within. Beware attending to the what ifs, the buts they haves, and the I just needs, for in understanding one's nature—and the nature of faith—one rests back into the knowledge they have all they will ever need. To think of a lowly daffodil growing up from the kerbside. A common, banal, and yet utterly triumphant sight. Is this not the modern worm for God, humbly doing only that which they can do from that which they have been given. Faith requires no more than itself, and doubt is but an adversary which proves the battle all the more worthy.

* * *

Exercise 8

Before undertaking this exercise sit for a few minutes and calm your thoughts.

This is an exercise that I've placed in much of my writing, even that which isn't necessarily spiritual, I call it a negative discursive meditation. Negative Theology holds that we can only know God by what we *don't* know about Him. Various theologians and mystics over the years have found ways to approach God by a continual act of reduction or negation. For instance, if some-or-other thought were to arise in one's mind when meditating on God that had some empirical standing, we would understand that to *not* be God for the fact we *can* know it. This type of thinking, then, is a negative working backwards (a reduction) to find something everlasting and deeper.

In this section, however, we have been talking about faith and the fact that there is no such thing as someone *without* faith. We all believe in something. This exercise, then, is to try to help us surmise or even realise what it is we have faith in. This exercise may take multiple days (possibly even weeks). Write down a list of things you consider to be important. For many it will be their children or partner, perhaps it's your car, house, job, pets, possessions, or hobbies. It doesn't matter what it is, if you consider it important, write it down. Once you have a list of things, each of which you know for a fact you consider to be important, select *one* as your theme of discursive meditation. Meditate on the theme chosen, but instead of simply turning it over and over again in your mind, try to reduce it. First ask 'Why *is* this important to me?' then, when you find some answer, ask why *that* is important to you, and so on until you can question no more. Perform one meditation session per day for each item on the list.

Journal your findings.

* * *

Humility and silence

So now we have an understanding of three clear things—grace, love, and faith. We should now also understand that each of these things *is* there for us all along, always will be, and always has been, and as such is within our reach via an act of personal choice, a decision between acceptance of what is or ignorance of what one wishes were. But there is a practical issue here that is difficult to address. Namely, how do we receive these gifts freely given?

If we were to receive a regular, everyday, material gift from someone, it follows that we would use our five senses and material body to do so. Picking up the gift, looking at it, maybe smelling or tasting it. However, God isn't material. He is beyond time and space. He is the Creator of all things. He is beyond the senses, beyond materiality. So how exactly do we receive a gift from He who is beyond the world? Or, even more strangely, we could ask ourselves—how can we receive a gift which is always there, always being given to us without condition? The how of this question is completely entwined with who we are, and how honest we are with ourselves. And so to receive we need to become 'worthy' to receive.

Here I turn once again to the Sermon on the Mount, as to draw in the first Beatitude that I left out earlier: *'Blessed are the poor in spirit: for theirs is the kingdom of heaven'*.

Much has been made of this simple line of Scripture, and in many ways, this is unsurprising as it is one clear place in the Gospels where we are given some hint as to what actions here and now will allow us entry to heaven. The Kingdom of heaven as that place unto which shall experience God's love fully and see Him face to face is the culmination of the grace and love we are to open ourselves to now.

For as it is said in Luke 17:21 *'For lo, the kingdom of God is within you'*, and as such, our relationship with God begins with ourselves, and we are to be 'poor'. There is a certain introspective loop found here which allows us some entry into 'what is to be done'. For we understand we are lost and not whole. That it is God alone that can suffice to fulfil us and make our lives content. God's Kingdom is already within us (the gift I have already spoken of), and we are to accept this gift.

Our acceptance of God's gifts begins by humbling ourselves. This virtue of humility has a direct relation to the aforementioned poverty of Matthew 5:3, *'The virtue of humility'*, Aquinas says, 'consists in keeping oneself within one's own bounds, not reaching out to things above one, but submitting to one's superior' (*Summa contra Gentiles*, 2018). And what are our 'own bounds'? They can be nothing other than the bounds which have always been and always will be, which is to say, the bounds of God's Kingdom within us. Let me simplify all this by returning to the metaphor of the corridor in the previous section.

We all have our own personal corridors, our own personal potential paths of communion with God. These paths—when left alone—are simple things, and at the end of them, we will find God's outstretched hand offering us grace, love, and faith. All we need to do is walk along the corridor and accept the gift. And yet, the majority of us don't do this. Many of us who *desire* to do this don't even do this, or struggle to do so. This is because we've dragged all kinds of junk into the corridor to block our path. Or, upon arriving at a blockage in the corridor—a fast car, a high-status job, some prideful event—we don't see it for what it is, but get waylaid and admire it for its own sake.

Yet there is something to be emphasised here. These 'things' which block our path to God aren't material in themselves. For the corridor I speak of is an internal corridor, it is our inner life. Yes, it may very well be that we appear to get distracted by worldly things such as money, careers, power, and status, but in truth we get distracted by our own relationship with them. One can happen to acquire a lot of money and still be charitable and giving; one can rise to the top of a career ladder and use that skill for good; one can become powerful and use their position to help, etc. But within such actions, it is clear that the material effects are secondary to some higher calling, a higher purpose. It is clear that such people would understand that worldly things can never fulfil them, and in this sense, they are still humble, they are still *poor*. To be *poor in spirit* has nothing to do with material poverty, it's right there in the third word 'spirit'. For it cannot be the case that poverty of this kind has anything to do with things and money, for if such was the case, then it would be that one's 'ticket to heaven' relied primarily on their relationship to the world as opposed to their relationship to God as if to say those who are financially poor were somehow automatically pious and faithful, and those of material wealth are automatically wretched and sinners—what folly!

To have spiritual poverty—and begin the ascent to the gifts always given—is to have an internal understanding that one is nothing, that one is completely ignorant, and that one should aspire with heartfelt, radical honesty to heal this ignorance. To be poor in this sense is not to own nothing, but to let nothing on you so as to allow space for He alone who can heal you. For if one is not internally poor then one is internally rich, their inner life is so full of pride, vanity, and thoughts of the world that there is no room for God's light and grace to enter. A follow-up question, then, is how exactly does one begin their entry into this internal form of poverty? How do we become poor in spirit and begin to clear out the corridor of our souls and see it with *eyes that can see*? For this, we need to become silent.

* * *

This begets another question—how do we become silent? And what exactly is this form of silence? We all apparently know what it means to be silent. We might declare that it's an absence of noise, or an emptiness of sound, or some such sensual idea of silence. We may think of a supermarket early in the morning before customers begin to arrive, a cinema just as the lights are going down, or a forest walk at twilight hours. All of which are stereotypical scenes where silence seems to invade our default state of noise. However, as supposedly calm and peaceful as we may find certain 'silent scenes' within life, I imagine we would be lying to ourselves if we declared them wholly silent. As the oft-repeated saying goes, *Wherever you go, there you are*, and, unfortunately for us the one thing which usually spoils a tranquil walk or beach sunrise is the noise in our own minds, the bustle of our own lives. These traits and habits, presumptions and idolisations, are in truth the noise that constructs all the obstacles we find within our personal corridors.

There is an underlying factor here that connects humility, silence, and the form of (spiritual) poverty we have been talking about, namely, honesty. In acting with humility we—to return to St Thomas' definition—understand ourselves from and within our bounds. To be silent is to accept reality as it is, without any noise or distraction. Finally, to be poor in spirit is to be honest about who you are and Whose will uphold you. To be silent is to be honest. More often than not, as soon as we make any kind of noise—be it the literal noise of idle talking, the idolisation of objects, or the inflation of a false, worldly self—we enter into a dishonest dialogue about just who it is we are, where we came from, and where are we are going. The noise that we make is in truth the noise of something or some worldly ideal being dragged into our inner corridor, blocking us from seeing God's gifts in all their simplicity. To fill the silence with our own wills is to believe we somehow know better than He who literally upholds all that is, and this, of course, cannot be.

This all leads back to the original question: Now that we understand that grace allows us to have faith, that faith is a gift freely given, and—to a large degree—a choice made via our own free will, how exactly do we make that choice? We begin with honesty as silence. In this silence, we can begin—very slowly at first—to recognise what the repetitive and consistent noise that appears in our corridor. We may even wish to introduce another metaphor here, based upon a common real-life disappointment, that of the scenic view or sunset, and this metaphor may allow us to see our own common noises.

Let's say we're looking forward to going hiking on a nature trail, the end of which is elevated and will allow us a beautiful view of the countryside. We've been working hard all week and as such are looking forward to this break from modern life. We settle ourselves to bed the night before and some of our stresses and worries dissipate. The morning arrives, we take a short drive, arrive at our destination and begin our hike, now with even more peace in our minds and hearts. As we ascend the trail we become more still, more at peace, and find many of our worries were minor and inconsequential, if not entirely nonsensical. We finally reach the peak, place ourselves on a bench, and have before us the beautiful, cathartic view we hoped for. And yet ... there's always something. A habit, ideal, or grievance which consistently manages to remain in our corridor and bar us from settling into our true selves and thus into God's voice. Perhaps we're still worried about our jobs? Our cars or homes? What are we going to be having for dinner? Maybe even how we look despite the fact no one else is around? It becomes clear in this moment of supposed perfect *external* silence that one develops a respect for the Truth of silence itself, which can only ever be internal. If our inner corridor is inflated and blocked then there can never even be a sunset or forest, for as soon as we begin to look at it our vision glosses over with the noise of the world.

Why is noticing these blockages, these things and thoughts that veil life as it is, so important? Because in our choice to notice them, we also notice that which we truly have faith in. After all, is pushed aside and the world allows us a moment's peace, who or what do we turn to as a way to figure it all out? Where is God here? Are we purposely hiding Him? Are we avoiding stepping closer towards Him by way of the common excuse 'Well, I'll head that way soon, but I just need to get this certain thing in order first'. The point is that all these *things*, which if only they were solved and no longer within our corridors, only *then* could we approach God with clarity in our step, is a backward way of looking at the situation. If we come to realise—via humbling ourselves in silence and poverty—that the empty, peaceful, and Right and Just corridor, complete with God's gift of faith is the foundation of all things, and that any further confusion or complexity is brought about solely by our own pride and oh-so-human ignorance, then we come to realise that our 'problems' are simply atop the contentment we seek via their solving.

There are no problems to be solved within the inner life, only ignorance we have conflated with mystery. The Lord and His gifts are before us, and as He is who upholds, directs, and causes all things, any such problems, and quandaries found within ourselves are merely attempted intrusions by the kingdom of the world into the Kingdom of God. And, if we *choose* the truthful clarity of faith over the falsity of worldly complexity, we shall be quick to see the corridor somehow clear itself, even though it was clear all along. But I don't want to avoid practicalities, so many books on God offer visions of beauty without any actual means to see them for yourselves, so I will spend some time here detailing how one can actually enter into this silence.

Noise and modernity

I've only lightly touched upon a certain factor of silence and humility which is critically overlooked, an element always holding an elusive position yet in reality moulding and mutating communication, the continual malicious interpreter that is *noise*. The world is a noisy place. So noisy, in fact, that we rarely notice the various forms of static sound which are humming away around us, the multitude of tiny clicks, drones, and buzzes which interfere with our inner life. Taken literally, materially, it's clear that we can whisk ourselves away from the excesses of noise by way of leaving the city or turning the volume down. Figuratively, however, and with respect to our relationship and communion with God, it's far more difficult—if not a lifetime task—to turn the noise down.

Let us once more think of this corridor between ourselves and God, the world and grace, self-will and His Will, noise, and peace. Viewed for what it is—a straight, simple path—it appears naive, bordering on flippancy in relation to God's greatness. And yet we are told in Matthew 18:3:

> *And said: Amen I say to you, unless you are converted, and become little children, you shall not enter into the kingdom of heaven.*

A child—then and now—is an image of innocence and powerlessness. They have little to no say in the shape their lives will take, and, despite the occasional rebellion or tantrum born from *pure* ignorance, the child is accepting of their helplessness. The inner life and path of a child are such that prior to social and worldly influence, they feel no need to drag all kinds of noise into their passage to God. It would make no sense to do so, for a child understands that no act of this kind will ever bring about a form of power which would render them truly sovereign. No amount of worldly noise is alone capable of proving to *children* of God that any other path is justified.

But the metaphorical child of Scripture, thrown into the world, develops into an adolescent, and eventually into a man or woman. The child walks innocent and whole, but as time passes and the noise of the world gets louder and the pressure starts to build, the child-becomes-teen and succumbs to the false promises of a thousand worldly parasites. With such noise comes schism, a fragmenting of silence into a plethora of false sovereignties, little pockets of static which lull one into a sense of power. Be it the humdrum of the rat-race, the synthetic twang of possessions, or the orchestral triumph of pride, whatever it is, it becomes apparent that noise soars, noise marks its territory, noise claims.

The difference between accepting and possessing (or grasping) is the difference between the child of God and the man of the world. Let's return to our corridor. The child accepts that which simply is, the gift of grace and faith which is understood as *given*. The (worldly) man doesn't humbly accept a position of poverty but attends to anything offered from the position of potential wealth. These things are not those which happen to be God-Willed into his life but are options for the taking, separate choices that can be made. To be a child is to accept the One and only choice; to be a man is to possess multiple choices. The fault, however, of these worldly men and women is that these choices are not choices at all, but mere distractions upon the only path there ever will be. God will forever be at the end of the corridor, He is the final destination for all things, and so what can any noise be but distraction from the perfection of silent communion with the Lord?

When we are asked to become as little children then, ironically it is not the case that we are being asked to run around and make noise, but, in understanding our powerlessness and fallen nature in the face of God's Will, we are asked to be silent before reality. The child doesn't make any noise, nor does he allow worldly chatter any jurisdiction, he simply uses his God-given eyes to see what is, as opposed to the maturation of wishing to see what is not. This of course draws up more questions. Why is it we are drawn into noise altogether? Who or what begets this noise in the first place?

The same fallen nature, which if admitted to and accepted in its fallibility and sin can allow us to understand God's mercy, is the very same nature that drew us away from it in the first place. If we can say anything about men—and the history of men writ large—it is that we think we know better. It doesn't matter who, what, when, or how, we always know better than anyone else. We are drawn to noise in a repetition that has not ceased since the Garden of Eden—in our futile attempts at worldly *possession*, we too grasp at the fruit from the Tree of Knowledge; Original Sin, as seen in all men, time, and time again, as the act of marking out what is ours, mine, and yours, is, ironically, very unoriginal.

But how-oh-how did all this noise, all this stuff get here? We ask. How, despite all doors being unlocked and with the free will to exit this darkest of noisy dungeons, did we get here? It is an idiotic, ignorant, and needlessly pig-headed question, and so it is of no surprise that it's our first port of call as humans. Covered in dirt from head to toe with all the means to wash, humans are quick to ask: 'How did I get dirty in the first place?' There is but one other thing which reaches the infinite besides God's forgiveness, and that is man's foolishness. However, if we wish to—as the saying goes—follow the finger pointing at the moon then there are two culprits, ourselves and the devil. We should understand by now how *our* own minds justify the noise of the world, but what of that latter, elusive figure, what role does God's primary antagonist—though not His 'evil opposite'—play in all this?

We return once more to free will and the fact that without it the entirety of theology falls flat. Grace, faith, and love (to name just a few gigantic facets of Christianity) are devoid of meaning in a world without the freedom to choose. What has this got to do with Satan/the devil? Satan was one of God's angels who rebelled against him prior to the creation of the world. But as God is ... God, Satan lost his 'battle' against the Lord and was banished to hell for all eternity. He, we are told in the Gospel of Luke, fell like lightning.

Satan, in his position of malice and rebellion, seeks only to encourage people to ignore God's commands and lead them to sin. *However*, the sin and fallen lifestyles Satan wishes people to choose are still—always, ultimately—their choice. Satan, then, is not solely responsible for all evil, for at the end of all pressures and influences is still our capacity to decide. But I believe that overt emphasis in either direction—'All evil is caused by Satan!' or 'All evil is caused by our own free will!'—is a grave simplification of a complex issue. Evil, as only ever a mutation and *defilement* of the Good (evil can never create), is so thoroughly intertwined into the world; it's often difficult to see where influences and choices begin. But let's look at just how Satan acts, and the limitations inherent within his nature.

We can imagine ourselves and our actions as being a crystal-clear glass of water. Before any external influences or internal 'rationalisations' have thwarted our simple path to God we are pure beings. We recognise God's love, we love Him back, and we walk down the corridor towards the Lord. Of course, it doesn't remain this simple. As we proceed through life all kinds of metaphorical dirt lands in our glass, and as an ink of darkness fouls the entire water, leaving us a little murkier, a little smogier. There's plenty of factors as to why such darkness is allowed to enter our lives. It may be that we've personally given ourselves over to pride or vanity in a momentary lapse of judgement. It may be that God has brought forth a worldly event to bolster a virtue such as courage, but we fell backwards into despair instead. Or it may be that a demonic 'voice' persuaded our hand to tip darkness into our lives itself.

I find this metaphor of water and ink (light and darkness) increasingly helpful, especially where ignorance is concerned. For given an articulate, good, and correct education, one would grow up understanding what it means and feels like to have one's own water clear. One would know that untainted, crystal water is how things are meant to be, and that in such a state God's light is allowed to flow uninterrupted. However, what the metaphor of the water allows us to see is that if one grows up and (falsely) matures within such a world that considers murky and tainted water as the norm, then such a person can be forgiven for conflating darkness with light. When, however, they come—via grace—to an understanding of the water prior to all fouling, to see the light for what it is, then beyond this moment any such defence of the darkness can only be from a position of wilful ignorance or pride.

Fear not, however, for God's mercy and love is infinite, and we need only reach out and accept it. To allow God's light to return fully to our lives—by way of prayer or Confession—in turn allows purification of the waters, for where light is darkness cannot be. These inherent definitions of darkness and light need to be emphasised for us to understand what is to be done. Where there is light, there cannot be darkness; for darkness to dissipate, light needs to enter. This brings forth an important question: Can light push darkness away, or do we need to dispel the darkness first, allowing a space for light?

The answer to this question is one of choice as opposed to conflict. Here we are speaking of the individual, personal inner lives of you and me. Each person has their own God-given free will, and acting as their own agent, a personal relationship to light and dark, good and evil. And so, it is not the case on the individual level that there is a non-influenced battle between light and dark, whereupon one will win out of sheer force or power. It is in fact the case that such a battle is—within the confines of our finite lifetime—beholden to our own affiliations and allowances. If we continue, despite our knowledge of the clear waters of God, to hold onto the false-truth of pride and murky water, then it is such that our own stubbornness is that which withholds the possibility of light from entering into our lives. If, conversely, we continue to ask for forgiveness, be as children, and remember our powerlessness, then we *open* ourselves to the simplicity of light and therein the impossibility of darkness. For where there is one—by definition—the other cannot be.

It is not, in itself, a difficult task to *become a child*. One need only be grateful for what is, what is freely given them; one need only *accept* and not take, thank and not ask; to defer their will over to God's, in the understanding that He is the only end, and the path ahead is either True-and-simple or false-and-complex.

How to be silent

So far we've looked at the landscape of faith, humility, and honesty with respect to silence. But just looking at and understanding how these things interconnect with one another isn't the same as actually practising silence. More often than not, books of this kind talk all the way home about the beauty and contentment of certain spiritual ideas without ever getting to the root of how to *do* them, or at the very least, how to begin to do them. Yet there's a difficulty in this for two reasons. First, it's far more difficult to discuss the simplest of things, for in their simplicity in addition to explanation tarnishes them. And secondly, silence is a certain form of positive-absence, and so I'm attempting to explain how to *do* that which one can't necessarily—by definition—do. In short, asking someone to *be silent is* to ask someone to *stop* making noise. The question still stands though, how is it we can *be* silent?

As we will now know, within the Christian context (and of course as God *is* real, in reality) silence is something much more than merely not being noisy. Silence is positive, silence is an opening, silence, as the oft-repeated saying goes, is deafening. It's this sense of silence having its own life, and being far more than the mere negation of noise, wherein we can learn how to be silent, and just what it is we are doing when we become silent. In moments of silence we aren't clearing our own internal corridors, but we are allowing what is there to be seen as it is. Reality is silence. Silence, as that which is before all noise, all civilisation, and all passions, is the foundation unto which we approach God.

> Only the silent hear and those who do not remain silent do not hear ... For leisure is a receptive attitude of mind, a contemplative attitude, and it is not only the occasion but also the capacity for steeping oneself in the whole of creation.
>
> (Pieper, *Leisure: the Basis of Culture*, 2009)

I will not speak of Pieper's concept of 'leisure' here (for he dedicates an entire book to it and I will do it a disservice), but I shall utilise his notion of silence as a contemplative attitude to further my cause, all of which shall slowly lead us towards a possible answer of How it is we can *be* silent.

To be silent is to be honest, to be honest is to be humble, and to be humble is the beginning of one's approach to God, as a child. To be able to hear we need to shut up. We basically never shut up, not really. One can witness the itch and impatience of a silent human, a fidgeting so apparent that they may as well have a megaphone in their hands. So to learn how to be silent, we need to understand why we struggle to not be silent, or why is it almost a virtue to be noisy all the time?

Noise is evident and noise is evidence. Noise, external and internal, is a proclamation to the world and to the self of a definite *thing*, some construction unto which we have projected importance. Externally, out in the world, we might rev our cars, fill our visual field with possessions, or declare each and every thought to an audience on social media. Internally, within our little corridors of beliefs and habits, we may desire to be seen, heard, or understood in a certain way. The root of most noise is ourselves and our own beliefs about our position in life. To be noisy is to assert our will against God's, it is to attempt to change what Will be into something which we simply want.

The first step then, to becoming silent, is, as I previously mentioned, to focus on those thoughts, ideas, and habits which arise in moments of generic silence. Finding ourselves on an empty hilltop, in a peaceful forest, or even sitting in a church, we come to realise that we're not truly *in* that place at all because our mind is quite literally elsewhere, creating a cacophonous nuisance of everything which is simple. We're worrying about money, possessions, food, work, and everything possible. We often find that when we come to understand one (supposed) problem and therein allow it to leave us be, another problem arises as if from nowhere. In noisy abidance to his own, individual will, man will never find peace.

It will appear almost suspiciously clear, but to be silent is simply *to be*, and in doing so allow and *open* oneself to God's Will which is, in truth, the only Will. As it is He who created and upholds all things, one's life will only be as it *is* and always has been with respect to that which the Lord has declared Right and Just. To be silent is to be content, for in silence one accepts reality as it is, as opposed to how they wish it could be; noise sets up a future which never was, and becomes disappointed on arrival.

Practically speaking, how then does one begin the practical matter of silence? Via a discursive relationship with noise. For one has few options when it comes to noise. Either you give into it, and enter into a lifetime of discontentment. Or you question it, prod at its origins, and discursively work backwards unto the roots of that which deafens us. What are we working backwards to? Well, God, of course.

* * *

Exercise 9

Before undertaking this exercise sit for a few minutes and calm your thoughts.

'All of humanity's problems stem from man's inability to sit quietly in a room alone', wrote Blaise Pascal and so that is exactly what I'm going to ask you to do. This exercise is one week long. Each day find somewhere you can be silent and undisturbed for 15 minutes. You are going to just *be*. Before beginning each 15-minute meditation, however, you are going to quietly, internally state 'Lord, I am here'. Then what? Then nothing. You sit in silence for the remainder of the time. Thoughts will try to intrude, the world will try to intrude, and you try as hard as you can to be fully silent for the 15-minute window. Perform this meditation every day for one week.

Journal your findings, if you wish.

* * *

Seeds

For me, this next section is of the utmost importance. Let me insert a little bit of biography to explain why. As I mentioned at the beginning, when I was younger I was raised in a Christian school and given the standard Christian education that one finds in the modern world. This amounted to little more than 'There's a big man in the sky!' and various repetitions of the 10 Commandments severed from their root. However, even with this education in my back-pocket one question always bugged me and is generally my go-to question for the majority of life's quandaries. 'What does this, practically speaking, amount to?' I always wanted to know why we were doing something, where it would lead us, and *what* we were building or growing. It's all very well abiding by certain rules and laws for the sake of truth alone, but if you haven't any idea what this actually amounts to it becomes far more difficult to stick to the path.

We now have the thorough, yet admittedly still abstract, foundation of Christian life. With grace, faith, and love as our structure, with silence and humility as our doorway of entry. All seemingly straightforward, and yet the question remains, what are we seeking to grow? I use the word *grow* specifically for its connection to that which is natural, that which is grown is done so organically and is not artificially built using various tricks. Growth, as anyone who's attempted to take up gardening will know, is a slow process of trial and error, or patience and learning. And it's this mentality we must take forward with us into life as Christians, we must think of ourselves as gardeners of the Spirit lest we fall into despair.

This may all seem a tad dramatic, but allow me to draw in the Parable of the Sower from Luke 8:5–11 to aid my cause:

> [5] *The sower went out to sow his seed. And as he sowed, some fell by the way side, and it was trodden down, and the fowls of the air devoured it.*
>
> [6] *And other some fell upon a rock: and as soon as it was sprung up, it withered away, because it had no moisture.*
>
> [7] *And other some fell among thorns, and the thorns growing up with it, choked it.*
>
> [8] *And other some fell upon good ground; and being sprung up, yielded fruit a hundredfold. Saying these things, he cried out: He that hath ears to hear, let him hear.*
>
> [9] *And his disciples asked him what this parable might be.*
>
> [10] *To whom he said: To you it is given to know the mystery of the kingdom of God; but to the rest in parables, that seeing they may not see, and hearing may not understand.*
>
> [11] *Now the parable is this: The seed is the word of God.*

There is no more apt passage of Scripture concerning the realities of the mission of each Christian than this one. For what he is to prioritise, the hurdles he will face, and the rewards he shall reap are all contained in these seven lines. Let us get back to gardening. Perhaps one seeks to grow some tomatoes, and in their naivete think it enough simply to purchase some seeds, throw them into the ground, water them a bit, and wait for their immense, perfectly ripe crop. The reality, even for such a basic and enduring plant, is far different. One needs to know just what *type* of tomato they're dealing with, what sort of soil it requires, what seasons and climates it grows in, and just how much water it needs. The terrain needs to be prepared for any seed to take root, and the same applies to the spiritual seeds we are seeking to grow within ourselves and others.

Yet there is more to this than a simple relationship of sower and seed, wherein we believe ourselves to be solely in the position of the sower, of he who casts out the possibility. For we too are seeds, or, more aptly, we too have a seed within ourselves, within our very being. Let me draw in further depths of theological language to help us understand what I mean. There are—for the Christian—two births. One is the generic birth of matter, where their body (often conflated entirely with 'themselves') is born. The second is more elusive, and happens within the inner life that I have been talking about, and it happens at Baptism. So as the blessed waters and the Spirit nourish our soul, leaving an eternal mark upon it, we are born anew into the Kingdom of God. In a sense, our first birth is of the world—our body is limited to the constraints of the world and of matter. But our second birth, wherein we are Baptised and accept Christ, is one which is connected to God's Kingdom, and isn't limited by the finitude of matter. So the answer to the question as to what it is we are to grow is our soul. But the growth of one's soul is a reciprocal task imbued with charity and silence.

As we are Baptised and thus born into the Kingdom as a *New Man*, we—in a much clearer sense—become seed and sower. First, we are a seed in the sense that we now have within ourselves a clear duty, *the imitation of Christ*. Many get almost short of breath at the idea of such a thing, the notion the mere possibility of their passing through the narrow gate is reliant on them literally imitating God Himself. And yet, for God to truly spread His message amongst man He Himself became man. The Path of the Christian is not outside of the bounds of possibility, for the Lord acted *as* man during His time on earth. And yet a seed needs to know its own limitations, its own pitfalls, and oversights. When we think back once again to the idea of growing even a simple tomato plant we can see that some are low maintenance, some are high maintenance. Some endure all weather, and some crumble under pressure. Some are reliable, some are temperamental. As we ourselves grow under the light of God, we need to first understand our own limitations before we seek serious imitation. For there is little use creating an abstract ideal to imitate (be it of a Saint or of Christ Himself) without realising that it is from ourselves and all our inherent faults that *we* must grow. One cannot pretend to be any other seed than that which they are—one will soon become unmotivated and fall into despair if one treats themselves as someone else.

The New Man

And so it is that men and women, upon receiving the Sacrament of Baptism, are reborn as new men and women, or the *New Man* and the *New Woman*. For me, this is one of the most critically overlooked and emphatically practical ideas tucked away in the depths of Christianity. Perhaps it is the case with almost all humans that they often desire a reset. They wish they could turn back the clock and try again. They wish they could be given another chance from the foundation of their newfound knowledge. Of course, in the modern world, where all material and all judgement has an everlasting trace, it appears that the notion of *actual* forgiveness—and thus a true reset—is non-existent. Yet, within Christianity and *from* the Kingdom of God, a True reset and purification is possible via the Sacrament of Baptism.

> *For the love of Christ controls us, because we have concluded this: that one has died for all, therefore all have died; and he died for all, that those who live might no longer live for themselves but for him who for their sake died and was raised. From now on, therefore, we regard no one according to the flesh. Even though we once regarded Christ according to the flesh, we regard him thus no longer. Therefore, if anyone is in Christ, he is a new creation. The old has passed away; behold, the new has come.*
> (2 Corinthians 5:14–17)

But to become new the old—as per the words of St Paul above—must pass away, which in turn means that *we* must allow the old to pass away. In much the same manner wherein darkness cannot exist where there is light, so too are the old and new unable to coexist. And, thus, it begs emphasis—one cannot become new if they continually cling to and possess the old. But this relationship with newness within ourselves is one and the same with light and darkness. It is an internal relationship with self-righteousness, self-justification, selfishness, and change. For as the seeds we are casting out need light and water (Goodness and Truth, freely given by God) to grow, so too does newness only arrive if we open ourselves to that which seeks to purify us. If we continue our lives as we are and as we were, then only secondarily can it be said that we haven't changed, for primarily it should be said that we simply haven't opened ourselves to the Lord, which is the foundation to any true change.

For of course, before all conversations and talks, all acts and tasks, one knows oneself to be in the right. And, once more, if it is that one is in the right, then what needs to change at all? Everyone else is wrong but you and I, of course. Everything one has done and will do has already been justified, and if queried, there is but an artillery of excuses and justifications at the ready. Make no mistake, all of us are already satisfied with ourselves as we are. And yet … what of that peculiar, quiet, internal voice which avoids even the most sly of the lies we tell ourselves? What of that overwhelming, silent urge to go to Mass and *be* better? What of our continual need to admit our wrongdoings before God in prayer and ask for forgiveness? How can it be that in the world we perceive ourselves to be just and whole, and yet when we turn our faces to the Lord we crumble into pieces and (hopefully) offer our hearts to Him? Is this not a double-life, one which needs to fold into itself as a means to purify the old and accept the new, however uncomfortable such newness might be?

And here it is where that oh-so-common misinterpretation of Christianity by modern man falls apart. For how can the idea that Christianity is an easy path remain when it is given that man needs to truly confront himself, and admit to his nothingness before God? For this is the meaning of Luke 9:57–58:

> [57] *As they were going along the road, someone said to him, 'I will follow you wherever you go'.*
> [58] *And Jesus said to him, 'Foxes have holes, and birds of the air have nests, but the Son of Man has nowhere to lay his head'.*

To follow Christ, truthfully, is to be temporarily homeless. For how can the *New Man*, who has forsaken the old world and his old self, have anywhere to lay his head when he understands that this world is pure folly? To change, to become new, isn't necessarily the *definite* giving over of everything, complete with entering into abject poverty. It *is*, however, willing to forsake everything for Christ. For in Baptism, one is incorporated into the body of Christ, and thus the door is opened to live life in imitation of Christ. One may have acquired all laws, rules, and knowledge available to them, but if they do not use it in abeyance for something Higher (the Will of God), then such a person remains within their own self-justification and righteousness, they use knowledge as if it were *theirs* and not freely given *to* them.

These discussions on being a seed, casting seeds, and becoming a *New Man* all relate to a well-known passage from the Gospel of Luke, specifically 17:21: '*The kingdom of God is within you*'.

If we are to begin our analysis of this scriptural excerpt with anything, it must be that which is implied via its emphasis on one certain kingdom over another. The distinction of the Kingdom of God as within us therein implies the separate kingdom of the world is elsewhere. So how are we to define that which is already within us? It can only be that which is *of* ourselves but not ourselves in complete form, namely, it is grace. Grace as the gift freely given unto those who open themselves in acceptance of their own incompleteness. In becoming a *New Man* then, it is strangely the case that we allow others' Will to speak through us, using our 'self' as a means for something higher. No longer shall we close ourselves off to the beauty of the new and the possible courage we may need to confront ourselves, no. In allowing our own internal seed to blossom and thus become a *New Man*, we need to open ourselves to the Lord.

For in this paradox we find ourselves within, wherein one wishes to change, to spiritually grow, to become a better person, and yet all they have as their means is themselves. To look upon the peculiarity of change then—How does one become a *New Man* if their only means is themselves as they already are? This is where God's Kingdom is needed, for there is that which is within us that we must open ourselves to as a means for something new to be born. If we are in darkness, or perhaps in a temporary state of darkness, no part of us *alone* can clear the horizon and allow ourselves to move forward. We need God's light. We cannot act alone to change who we are, to do so would be an impossibility. We need help. We need Christ.

Before we can help others (cast seeds) we need to help ourselves (become a seed), before we can help ourselves we must learn to accept help from God. It is a matter of mediation, for how could we possibly cast or even hold pearls if we continue to be swine? And so this leads me in a full loop, right back around to the beginning of this piece wherein I stated quite matter-of-factly that I would tell you what it is we, as Christians, are growing. I have only tip-toed around the reality that to grow that which is desired, the most obvious of all things, that is, the Good and the Truth, one needs to be able to see themselves for who they truly are. For as it stands, most of us (myself included), march into our gardens with the utmost motivation. We plant our crops within sight of the sun, we water them consistently. But in our ignorance we haven't even begun to de-weed the soil, let alone turn it over. We all seek to approach God, but in understanding that the 'self' of 'ourselves' which shall eventually (possibly) reach God can—by definition—not be ourselves at this moment, we must understand the need to let go, to purify. For if we were in such a state of being as to be able to live fully in accordance with God's Will, meeting Him where and when we can, then we would already be doing such a thing. As it is, we understand ourselves to be far from the Lord, yet it is only ourselves—and our own understanding of ourselves—which bars us from nearing Him.

Our potential as a Christian

This may have one asking themselves, 'If I am a seed, then what is it I am growing into?' Ultimately this is a question of teleology, of means and ends—what is it the Christian is attempting to become? Almost paradoxically, a Christian is always attempting to become nothing more than a better Christian. One is always seeking to follow Christ, but as one grows and matures, they are attempting to do so without as many slip-ups, and without diverting possibly as drastically as they did when they were younger. This leads me to a practical (yet still abstract) method as to how it is one is to become a better Christian. Once more looking at that difference between the kingdom of the world and the Kingdom of God.

For in a metaphorical sense, there is already a part of us which has its foot (so to speak) within the Kingdom of God, namely, our soul. Our individual souls are that which God breathed into us at the moment of conception, and can be thought of as that emphatically *divine* part of us which therefore is already eternity. The eternal life—or, the afterlife—which we think of as far away and a long time coming, is already within us and we are already within it. For as our material bodies—complete with their five senses—are merely the means or tools unto which our consciousness acts, it is such that the only time we *have to act* is when we have our body, for our soul cannot act of its own accord. And so when we are alive within the kingdom of the world and acting from our material/physical bodies, our actions are made (roughly) for or against the faithful and grace-filled nature of our soul, itself part of the Kingdom of God (it is divine).

It is in this relationship of mediation, and thus man's peculiar ontological position of being matter and spirit, wherein we find our answer as to how to practically act. For in the knowledge that we are of spirit, and that upon death it is not the case that our bodies are us entirely, and as such our soul shall continue on, wherein we find the key as to how to act. In all moments, duties, and tasks of the world, one should act—and therein grow—in the presence and foresight of the Kingdom of God to come. A Christian should act for the sake of his soul and therein for the sake of Christ and God. The soul, as that mediating key between one kingdom and another should remain the central focus of all actions. In eating certain foods we may ask how it shall affect our material weight, or query how a drug may affect our mind, but rarely do we ask if undertaking a certain action as opposed to another will have a better or worse effect on our souls and thus our eternity.

In each moment we are called to keep the Kingdom at the forefront of our thoughts and minds, paying attention to life and experience in such a way that we develop a means to consistently place it before us. There is a clumsily—and largely tongue-in-cheek—repeated phrase: 'What would Jesus do?' A saying which, for those familiar with the Gospels and a little theology, places unfathomable requirements onto those even attempting to partake in this idea seriously. In attempting to do what Jesus Himself would do, we are creating an idealised version of Him, and thus losing ourselves to become like Him. When the reality is that we have each been given a soul (a piece of the divine) by God unto which we are individually beholden. A more helpful statement might be something such as 'What is it within me which is stopping me from acting for the betterment of my soul?' Admittedly this is a tad heavy-handed, so perhaps we could change it to 'How will you explain this choice, this action, to God?'

It is a harsh question, and much more poignant than the question of what Jesus (literally God) would do, standing before God. How will you answer your actions and non-actions? What will you say or feel when presented with the fact you repeatedly did that which you knew was wrong for your sole benefit? What will you say when all your excuses fall away and you're left with only your own useless pride? In the times when you knew right from wrong, just from unjust, good from evil, in these moments when one acted for self or not at all, what shall be your answer? And it is from this question, of knowing that one's soul—and thus ourselves—are already within the eternity we *feel* is so far off, from which we can begin to act with a needed impatience.

In the sense that the soul already *is* eternal, and as such we are already a foot-in-the-grave and a lean into the afterlife, we need to instil the idea that it is far later than we think. Life is but a blink. Even the average, so-called lengthy life of 70–80 years, is put a spark between two eternities, and how shall we defend our actions which are usually little more than known folly? We need to act as if the words of Mark 1:15 were etched into our hearts!

> *And saying: The time is accomplished, and the kingdom of God is at hand: repent, and believe the gospel.*

The time of our bodily, worldly lives is that unto which we have to accomplish, but as for the reality of our soul, therein the Kingdom of God is already at hand. There is and can be no such thing as patience, a break, or a moment to collect oneself, if we are to follow Christ and act to save ourselves the time to do so is *now*, simply because now already and always is eternal.

Rich and poor

The Rich Man

In this chapter, I'd like to discuss some of my favourite sections of the Gospels, and what I also consider to be the most practically applicable analogies found within Scripture, that is, the themes of poverty, possessions, rich, and poor. I have already given you a taste of my own reading of the meaning of 'poverty', but herein I would like to develop an extensive understanding of what it means to be both rich and poor in emphatically Christian terms. Here I will place the full story, Mark 10:17–31, the story of Jesus and the rich young man:

> *And when he was going forth into the way, a certain man running up and kneeling before him, asked him, Good Master, what shall I do that I may receive life everlasting? And Jesus said to him, Why callest thou me good? None is good but one, that is God. Thou knowest the commandments: Do not commit adultery, do not kill, do not steal, bear not false witness, do no fraud, honour thy father and mother. But he answered, and said to him: Master, all these things I have observed from my youth. And Jesus looked on him, loved him, and said to him: One thing is wanting unto thee: go,*

> sell whatever thou hast, and give to the poor, and thou shalt have treasure in heaven; and come, follow me. Who was struck sad at that saying, went away sorrowful: for he had great possessions.
>
> And Jesus looking roundabout, saith to his disciples: How hardly shall they that have riches, enter into the kingdom of God! And the disciples were astonished at his words. But Jesus again answering, saith to them: Children, how hard is it for them that trust in riches, to enter into the kingdom of God? It is easier for a camel to pass through the eye of a needle, than for a rich man to enter into the kingdom of God. Who wandered the most, saying among themselves: Who then can be saved? And Jesus looking on them, saith: With men it is impossible; but not with God: for all things are possible with God. And Peter began to say unto him: Behold, we have left all things, and have followed thee. Jesus answering, said: Amen I say to you, there is no man who hath left house or brethren, or sisters, or father, or mother, or children, or lands, for my sake and for the gospel, Who shall not receive a hundred times as much, now in this time; houses, and brethren, and sisters, and mothers, and children, and lands, with persecutions: and in the world to come life everlasting. But many that are first, shall be last: and the last, first.

I didn't want to include such a long, uncut section of the Gospels, but I found that there isn't a line here which can even be considered transitory. This story in its entirety is about wealth from the Kingdom, and within it we can find a (heavenly) wealth of information and guidance regarding the falsity of worldly riches, let's dive in.

We begin with the acknowledgement that there is a connection between our understanding of what it means to be 'poor', and how it is we are to receive life everlasting. A question which rarely has a clear answer (So how is it we get to heaven?), within this story gains one. Prior to adhering to the Christian notion of poverty Christ tells us to abide by the 10 Commandments. Before we get hasty and begin asking for tasks, duties, and the means to bolster our virtue, Christ draws us back to the basics of Scripture. Before we are given the means to travel further with our desire to be virtuous, Christ holds us to court as to whether or not we're abiding by the basics first; we need to learn to walk before we can run, because when children run, more often than not they end up falling over, getting sullen, and begin to sulk about life. Yet it is the case in this story that the young man has observed these commandments since his youth, and as such Jesus—taking him at his word—tells the young man that then only one thing is wanted of him, sell whatsoever thou hast, and give to the poor, and thou shalt have treasure in heaven; and come, follow me.

So here we see a reference to two types of treasure (one implied by the other), we have the *treasure in heaven* and the implied 'treasure of the world'. We are entering into a discussion regarding 'treasure' and thus wealth, and therein what it means to *be* rich or poor with respect to God. The young man, however, was struck with sadness for he had great possessions, and it is here wherein it becomes clear that it cannot be the case that we are speaking of generic treasures and possessions such as gold, jewellery, and property, for the young man—though, perhaps begrudgingly—could quite easily sell all his worldly possessions and follow Jesus. For it can only be that something of the sort which can have interaction with the soul could bar one from receiving the treasures of heaven; it cannot be material itself which blocks one from the heavens, but only our internal relationship to it.

The key, to this story and to the Christian virtue of poverty, is found within the word possession. I am not speaking here about demonic possession, but the general idea of what it is to possess. If one believes they possess something, they have grasped it, or even taken it. Then that person believes that such a 'treasure' is somehow cut off from existence and is solely theirs. Of course, this can never be true because all things are upheld by God's Will, and the declaration of possession is in truth the false belief that one's own will upholds something. In such a case, that which we possess truly possesses us, and we continue to retain an existence of defence, bordering, and suspicion where our possessions are concerned. The young man who was asked to give up his possessions, then, is in truth not asked to give up his material items, but only the possessive internal relationship he has with them. He may, practically speaking, be able to hand them over to the poor, but it will likely be the case with many that one's heart and mind would still believe it possessed them. Jesus isn't asking the young man to alter his relationship with the world and worldly treasure, for Jesus understands how fickle the kingdom of the world is. No, Jesus is asking the young man to develop a relationship with the Kingdom of Heaven, here and now, so that he may pass through the narrow gate.

Poverty

From this idea of what it means to be rich, or to be the allegorical 'rich man', we can begin to discern just what exactly is meant by poverty. To be poor or to live 'in poverty' in the Christian sense is actually a moral tightrope walk. The rope and walk itself is a sincere and humble existence in line with God's teaching, on one side lies naivete and self-harm, and on the other side overt pride.

First and foremost we need to once more centre on the fact that our lives are not *ours* in the common sense we think they are. Once again, they are God's and upheld by His Will. Therefore, our own wills (which are free) play a role in so much as we have a choice as to whether or not we live in agreement with God's Will or consistently rebel against it. Though it appears in such a sense that we are therefore not free—for what Will be is already known by God—this is not the case, for what *will* be is that which has been *ordained* by God, our own, self-willed actions, are therein allowed by God to come to pass. The point is, however, that in relation to the teachings found in Scripture, and the teachings set out by Jesus Christ, it is relatively clear to us how we are to behave and act if we are to follow God's Will. So why, then, do I claim that the doctrine of poverty is so precarious? To answer this I turn to Matthew 6:1:

> *Take heed that you do not do your justice before men, to be seen by them: otherwise you shall not have a reward from your Father who is in heaven.*

Poverty, though not necessarily the *clearest* place one might perform their 'justice before men', is, however, one doctrine where one may find oneself lying to oneself, conflating external worldly acts with a quantified internal change. Which is to say, poverty is often mistaken for a virtue, which is truly erroneous for a virtue to be something honourable or praiseworthy in itself. In comparison to other Catholic virtues poverty *can be* a relatively empty act. For to have temperance one must act against their passions, to have courage one needs to confront agony, pain, or danger, and to act justly one must find a point of moderation, actively placing oneself aside. But what of poverty? In the face of these virtues it is clear where poverty could fall short, for there is no need internally to confront anything at all, to unblock or overcome that which shadows our path to God. It may be the case that externally we live frugally, eat cheaply, drive an old car, reuse and reduce, and believe we take no more than we *deserve*. And yet, in our hearts, it could very well be the case that there are deep yearnings for the latest fashions or trends, that in certain moments we trick ourselves into 'needing' certain items, we self-justify the purchase of various objects perhaps even using Christianity as our defence. Out in the world we make our justice apparent before other men and women, but within ourselves (where space for the Kingdom should have been made) we covet that which we believe we lack even more for its absence. The space made by clearing external riches only leads us to feel more internally poor; we haven't made a space for God, but our signalling made it slightly more difficult for us to see Him.

On the one side you have this form of pride, overt and external acts of worldly poverty performed before others. Yet, on the others is naivete, forgivable yet harmful. Springing from a childish simplicity that the Lord Shall Provide—though he may very well, it shall be His decision—one decides to throw away that which the Lord has already provided. Though such acts are not as external and self-centred as the others, they arise from spiritual arrogance and pseudo-asceticism. This is why pride is the most pervasive of all sins. One can become prideful about the size of their house, the speed of their car, or the number in their bank account. But equally, one can become prideful about how many times they go to Confession, how little they own, or even how often they read the Bible. And yet if one is sat, eyes glued to the Gospels, but thinking 'Boy, I do hope people find out how often I read the Bible!', such is the case that they are no different than one who boasts of their possessions.

It all drifts back to Eden, to Original Sin, and what it is to believe one possesses something. As Eve possessed the apple (and therein the knowledge of Good and Evil), so too do we believe ourselves to truly possess things. Our house is ours, we *earned our* money, I read the Bible X amount of times per week, my confessions are mine, etc. We grasp everything and believe it to be ours, indefinitely. Whereas, in Truth, *nothing is ours*, not even our own lives are ours in any real sense. God's Will upholds *all*, and so all is His and comes *from* Him, we are but to be thankful for what we have received and our borrowing for our short stint within the world. To be poor, to *live* and exist in poverty is to understand life in such a way that one never *possesses*, what is *one's* is everyone's; one is in poverty because they are poor in spirit and understand that *possession* is mere folly, to possess is fill space where the Lord may enter, and yet now the passage is blocked by your own hand, a hand which doesn't wish to let go of emptiness as to make way for the fullness.

To be poor is to be rich.

Charity

All of this talk on wealth, riches, and poverty leads us to one of the most practical, Christian virtues—charity. Outside of other generic comments regarding what it means to be a Christian, one commonly repeated ideal is that a Christian is charitable. However, much like many other terms which have long-since drifted into a solely material understanding, the concept of 'charity', too, has become little more than a modern afterthought.

If we are honest with ourselves, *charity*, within the modern world, is usually little more than the pocket-change being nonchalantly thrown into the bucket next to checkouts. Perhaps it's a raffle we enter, still holding the prospect of personal gain, or maybe it's an act of helping wherein deep down we know we're scoring points to be used later. I tend to hold a fairly pessimistic view of the world, so it may very well be the case that most people are far more selfless than my thoughts here allow, but I've yet to see it. Whether this is true or not, the modern appreciation of charity—though not necessarily incorrect—falls quite far from the mark of what it truly means to be charitable, or to adhere to the virtue of charity. Once again, I will turn to a chapter from Scripture—Mark 12:41–44, often known as *The Widow's Offering*:

> *And Jesus sitting over against the treasury, beheld how the people cast money into the treasury, and many that were rich cast in much. And there came a certain poor widow, and she cast in two mites, which made a farthing. And calling his disciples together, he saith to them: Amen I say to you, this poor widow hath cast in more than all they who have cast into the treasury. For all they did cast in their abundance; but she of her want cast in all she had, even her whole living.*

I feel that if we are to understand this once more solely materially, the surface-level reading of this chapter is fairly straightforward. Those who are materially rich will find in their lives no additional stresses and troubles if they throw in lots of money, for they can afford to without any discomfort to themselves. The poor widow, however, it is clear can likely *afford* to put in nothing at all, and yet she puts in quite literally everything she has, a true act of empathy. Materially speaking, it could be read as a study of wealth or even risk. But if we are to look deeper, we can pry out a greater meaning of what it is to be charitable.

We begin again, with those who are rich, those who cast in much. The simplicity of Mark's language allows us little context. However, if such people are rich and can afford to cast in much without any alteration to their way of life, in what sense can this be considered charity? If it is the case that voluntarily offering any amount of money (which one can afford) into a pot one isn't obliged to offer into is the definition of charity, then we've quantified virtue into a case of more or less. It is clear that in the case of those who are rich that no sacrifice is made, their offering will change nothing of their lives, and is undertaken in the manner of modern charity, a quick launch of loose coins to appease one's own sense of self-worth. For is it not almost tragic that the majority of modern acts of charity are in truth primarily beneficial to the giver and not the receiver? We offer up loose change because it's practically worthless and takes up space in our wallet, we donate *only* the clothes we no longer care for, and we donate only the food which was dropped at the back of our cupboards. But when we turn our gaze to the widow, what do we see?

The 'poor widow', as per the context of Scripture, is socially and economically found upon the lowest rung of society. In the day of the Gospels, a widow would become reliant on others for many things, a *poor* widow doubly so. And yet, this woman whom we have come to understand as those who seemingly are the poorest amongst us, is she who offers *everything* she has. If we are to read this literally then it is the case she offers up possibly any money she has, likely going without food or heat due to this act of sacrifice. If we are to read this metaphorically, then perhaps it is the case that such a person gives up their time to help others when they could be gaining money, or maybe they feed others and go hungry themselves. The widow's offering comes not from a place of social signalling, appeasement, or etiquette, but from a place of sacrifice.

As such, charity without sacrifice is of a quantitative, calculated sort. An offering already figured to cause no disruption to one's comfort. Charity *with* sacrifice, however, is of a qualitative sort. In such a case—as with the widow—one places themselves in the position of the others they seek to help and support, and in offering up everything they have, become as equals in the strife and suffering of others. It is at one and the same time an act of personal sacrifice and faith. For in offering up that which will disturb our worldly comfort (as a way to comfort others), we have faith in the Lord that He will direct all things to their correct place and all will receive the rewards they deserve. Also, such acts are those of the humble, of those who understand that all is not *theirs* in a *possessive* sense, but all is the Lord's, and as such should be used solely for the betterment of all His children. Who are we to proclaim this and this and this are *mine* when countless others are starving? Not wanting to darken the tone and yet needing to, if we are to *take Christianity seriously*, then what will one say on the day of judgement for all those times one gorged themselves on food as others starved? Those times one needlessly turned up the heating as others froze? Those countless times we threw another coin into our pile for the sake of its growth whilst others had nothing? What will our answers be when we, and our possessive internality, is set before the Lord?

Charity, as a virtue, is so much more. If we are to turn to the Catechism, charity is defined as *'the theological virtue by which we love God above all things for His own sake, and our neighbour as ourselves for the love of God'*, this is a far cry from putting some spare change into a tub or baking some cakes for a fair. In being charitable, then, first we love God. But with regard to what it means to *be* charitable, why is loving God of the foremost urgency? The choice (once again) between Love of God or love of something else (in truth, nothing), is the only choice we have. To love God after something else is actually to love something else first, in such a case one is literally putting something of the world *before* He who made all things possible altogether. Utter absurdity. In this True kind of charity we draw ourselves closer to the form of love which God shows to us, namely, unconditional love. To truly *be* charitable one needs to work towards changing their inner life as to remove all judgement and worldly decisions and to make way for God's light, thereby seeing all men from and with a position of poverty. All are spiritually poor and all need this kind of non-judgemental love.

The primary difficulty is to 'love our neighbour as ourselves'. For this is charity in the practical sense. Beginning from a foundation of loving God, one moves through to the world choosing to remain with grace, and therein acting in such a way that we interact and think of others as if they were ourselves. This idea, which we are commonly taught in school under the plateau 'Treat others as you wish to be treated', often falls short of the mark within the modern world because the theological foundation of loving God (and God's love) has been removed. In a specifically *worldly* sense, 'treating others as you wish to be treated' can mean a whole manner of things. Many people may be naturally selfish, others blind to certain sufferings, and many may simply be ignorant of their shortcomings. All of these result in a treatment of charity that is lopsided, often covertly in favour of one's own biases or even prejudices.

But what if we were to treat others as we wish to be treated *from* the foundation of God's love? How does this change our appreciation of what it is to be charitable? First and foremost, we can turn to passages such as Galatians 3:28: *'There is neither Jew nor Greek: there is neither bond nor free: there is neither male nor female. For you are all one in Christ Jesus'*; or John 13:16: *'Amen, amen I say to you: The servant is not greater than his lord; neither is the apostle greater than he that sent him'* and realise that *all men are created equal*, and we are not to place any man lower or higher than any other; all prejudice, judgement, and bigotry has first to be removed. A task that in itself may take a lifetime. And yet, if we are to view others from the foundation of the Lord, that is, *as children*, then what is it that we see? No longer shall we look upon men and women as builders and sculptors of their own destinies who actively imbue the world with sin and greed (though this may be the case). No, in a non-condescending way, all men and women become children, scuttling around the world lost and confused, without the one True anchor which can make them whole. Their sins and faults are regularly a matter of being misguided, their secularism a tragic matter of pride, and their selfishness but a false island of stability to keep them afloat amidst their blind hubris. We become willing to give up anything for another because we now see that other person as they truly are, a brother or sister in Christ, a fellow human being who also (by their very Nature), whether they know it or not, is seeking the Lord. And in our acts of charity, we put all others before us because we seek—to quote Rafael Cardinal Merry del Val y Zulueta's *Litany of Humility*: 'That others may become holier than I, provided that I may become as holy as I should, Jesus, grant me the grace to desire it'.

There can be no sense of 'spiritual competition' if all are equal under God, and therefore, how holy one or another shall become is down to that which the Lord has offered them to freely accept (if they choose to), we, as fellow brothers and sisters in Christ, are there in dutifully obliged to help share the Love of God where we can. This is the truth of charity. We become nothing beneath the Lord and seek nothing of the world. We come to truly internalise that all that is, both of ourselves and others, is thanks to the Love of God, and so what else *could there be to do* but also to Love His Creation?

Light and darkness

Light and love

> *I am the light of the world: he that followeth me, walketh not in darkness, but shall have the light of life.*
>
> (John 8:12)

There is perhaps no more archetypal symbol of goodness than light. In fact, it may possibly be argued that light is the original symbol. This a drastic claim, but when one thinks about both Scripture and material reality, light is that which makes both possible. *Let there be light* is found at the beginning of Genesis, for before this the earth was without form and darkness was upon the face of the deep. Formless and dark, entirely unknowable, it is only from the illumination of light that anything can *be* for a man. And so it is that our material reality is beholden to light, both in appearance and possibility. It would not be possible to witness the splendour of the world without light, and the world itself and all its fruit equally could not grow without the nourishing properties of light. The light had to be before all things for them to be at all.

It is this basic reality of light that will allow us to unfold its symbolic meaning. Put simply, light is that which illuminates and that which nourishes. Of course, as with all things, and most emphatically with all symbols, these two standard meanings find their revealed, deeper understanding in relation to God. As it is that light illuminates and nourishes, so too—as the course of such gifts—does God. And yet, as we can see from the example given in Genesis, light (as is the case with most things in life) can only be understood by comparison with its negative, darkness. Even in Scripture, we are to understand that darkness was upon the face of the deep prior to the coming of light, and how could it have been otherwise—for if there is light, there cannot be darkness.

First then, let's look at the deeper symbolic meaning of light with regard to illumination, and what it means for light to dispel darkness. Beginning *in* the dark, one would feel insecure, unable, and lost. In the material sense, darkness cuts off our ability to see and thus (to a certain degree) know. Stretched further, to be 'in the dark' entirely is to have our senses cut off entirely, becoming a floating mind without anything to grasp. Light, then, is a metaphor for life, for without it, we have nothing but an empty existence of pure confusion. And yet light—at least in terms of human existence—is a matter of choice, even where the world is concerned. We need to plant our crops where we know the light will get to them. We need to open the curtains to let light in. We need to turn on the light or bring in a candle where no natural light can penetrate. Light, then, both materially and symbolically, is a decision. For even in the most scorching desert, where not an inch of shade can be found at all that abounds in the fullest light, we can still decide to bow our heads and turn our backs, using the shade of our own bodies as an alternative.

And so it is symbolically, with man and his relationship to God. In the simplest sense, as one plants crops in clear light, an individual can 'plant' their life amidst places, people, and atmospheres they know are full of light—church, family, friends, and prayer. Equally, when a house is known to be dark, or a friend is wallowing in thick despair, one may bring their light as a candle of the Word *into* the darkness, momentarily dispelling it. Or one may arise each day, possibly unable to ignore the sufferings and falls of the world, and yet instead of rolling around in the dark, they decide to arise and open the curtains, allowing God's light to fall upon all that is in their path.

And yet, as darkness cannot be where there is light, so too can light not be where there is darkness. The two cannot exist together, one must rule, even if moment-to-moment one's focus flicks between them.

There is no greater passage of Scripture to understand this idea than Christ's temptation in the wilderness found in the Gospel of Matthew 4:1–11, which I will quote here in full:

> *¹ Then Jesus was led by the spirit into the desert, to be tempted by the devil.*
>
> *² And when he had fasted forty days and forty nights, afterwards he was hungry.*
>
> *³ And the tempter coming said to him: If thou be the Son of God, command that these stones be made bread.*
>
> *⁴ Who answered and said: It is written, Not in bread alone doth man live, but in every word that proceedeth from the mouth of God.*
>
> *⁵ Then the devil took him up into the holy city, and set him upon the pinnacle of the temple,*
>
> *⁶ And said to him: If thou be the Son of God, cast thyself down, for it is written: That he hath given his angels charge over thee, and in their hands shall they bear thee up, lest perhaps thou dash thy foot against a stone.*
>
> *⁷ Jesus said to him: It is written again: Thou shalt not tempt the Lord thy God.*
>
> *⁸ Again the devil took him up into a very high mountain, and shewed him all the kingdoms of the world, and the glory of them,*
>
> *⁹ And said to him: All these will I give thee, if falling down thou wilt adore me.*
>
> *¹⁰ Then Jesus saith to him: Begone, Satan: for it is written, The Lord thy God shalt thou adore, and him only shalt thou serve.*
>
> *¹¹ Then the devil left him; and behold angels came and ministered to him.*

Behind the scenes here we have a relationship between darkness and light, and how the relationship between these two 'forces' *must* be. We may call it good or evil, virtue or sin, or light and dark, but it will always stand that such forces cannot coexist. Christ's temptation allows us to perceive the peculiarity of darkness, its comforts, and false certainty. First it is such that the devil wishes for Christ to turn stones to bread, or to transform the world into the heavens. Second, Jesus is tempted to leap from the pinnacle of the temple and be saved by angels, thereby testing the efficacy of light against the criteria of the world. And third, Jesus is offered—by the devil—the kingdom of the world. Many often focus on this trifecta of temptation with regard to their worldly focus, for each subverts the heavens to the world, therein falsely attempting to make the devil become God.

Yet there is something deeper at work, an atmosphere of confident darkness which, momentarily, overthrows all possibility of light. For, once again, where there is darkness there cannot be light, by definition. Yet it is not that Jesus has been *overcome* by darkness, as much as in His nature as God-man He is still open to that which all men are, namely, one's individual battle against evil. And so herein this section of Matthew we see not Good versus Evil, but a battle against evil as to *open* the door for light to enter. The denouncement of the devil and the Glory of God *over* each temptation *pushes* darkness away, and as each temptation is fought away it becomes all the more possible for light to enter. And so it is, that as the darkness is cleared and the devil leaves it becomes *possible* for angels (light) to enter and minister to Christ.

Spiritual warfare

And yet with this discussion of the light and the dark, of Good and Evil, we need to practically return to ourselves and the world we inhabit. It is perhaps the strangest of quandaries that we think all men and women know what is Good, and yet enter into Evil. Perhaps it is the case that many are entirely ignorant of what it is to *be* Good, and as such cannot be blamed for their blindness. However, there is undoubtedly that spirit within us and now written within a culture which defines itself as morality, or for our discussion Christian morality. There is a well-defined system and understanding of what it is to be a Good person. Some may turn this question over in their minds and declare that such a debate is not settled. But I hold that those with faith, those who study the Bible, and those who have heard the teaching of Jesus Christ in all their simplicity *know* what it is to be Good. So it is I believe the question of importance is now how to be Good, but merely why we are not. Why, in the face of basic moral virtues such as charity, hope, courage, and love, do we time and time again fall prey to selfishness and greed, despair, cowardice, and hate? Why do we *do* that which we know we should not do? Here we turn once more to Scripture, to Romans 7: 13–20:

> *Did that which is good, then, become death to me? Certainly not! But in order that sin might be exposed as sin, it produced death in me through what was good, so that through the commandment sin might become utterly sinful.*

> *We know that the law is spiritual; but I am unspiritual, sold as a slave to sin. I do not understand what I do. For what I want to do, I do not do it. But what I hate, I do. And if I do what I do not want to do, I admit that the law is good. In that case, it is no longer I who does it, but it is sin living in me that does it.*
>
> *I know that nothing good lives in me, that is, in my flesh; for I have the desire to do what is good, but I cannot carry it out. For I do not do the good I want to do. Instead, I keep on doing the evil I do not want to do. And if I do what I do not want, it is no longer I who does it, but it is sin living in me that does it.*

Here we see that it *cannot* be that the Good in us can die, for as our souls are divine and breathed into us by God, so too is it that imprinted within our very being is an innate understanding of that which is Good, Righteous, and Just. What is a *pang* of conscience but that darkly silent acknowledgement that one has acted against God and is in danger of falling from the narrow path altogether? The Good cannot die for what is Good shall always be. But the production of sin as the mutation and bastardisation of this Good is all Evil can ever hope to achieve. For the darkness is nothing and has nothing of itself, a world which in its entirety is understood to be dark could not be understood at all. It is only with the coming of Light and Goodness that we can see the darkness for what it is. There is no path of sin, only erroneous footing. We know in our hearts who we are to be and what we are to do, and the symptoms of sin are therefore that of despair, anxiety, worry, and hatred. In our missing of the mark, in our lapses of attention, we understand at the level of the soul we have wronged that which is Good by the very fact we are *born* with the Good in our hearts and very being.

But in that final paragraph of Scripture (Romans 7: 18–20), such writing has never arrived closer to the great folly and paradox of man's fallen nature. I know what I must and should do, and yet I do not do it. Is this not the contradiction that defines what it *is* to be human at all? And yet there is always hope. We find it here in the acceptance that the sins we commit are living in us as something, not of ourselves. Not some split personality or detached voice, but a grovelling, charismatic sly persuasion seeking by false promises to lead us to false rewards. To return to that *pang* of conscience, that shrieks deep within our hearts as we commit ourselves to a path other than the one that shall save us. One would not blame any man for going mad if they were to meditate on this paradox. But there is still more hope.

It is not the path of man to overcome this paradox in its entirety. As in strength and courage doubt begets a greater faith, so too—as we have seen—in silence and humility does contradiction beget growth. To sin is, by definition, *to miss the mark*. And *from* such acts, from standing vertical once more and casting aside our pride we are free to look back upon our falls as moments of learning. Each lapse and trip is a reminder of our inherent fallibility, our humanness, and our *need* for the Lord's unifying love. And as it is with doubt one must be wary to not ascribe the fall to more reality than it has and continue soaring downwards in an act of prideful sunk cost. One must fall and rise, leaving behind them that which caused them to fall in the first place. There is but one thing the devil and Evil do not and *cannot* have, and that is humility. We mustn't fall and believe ourselves better than falling, we must not sin and believe ourselves better than error, and we must not act and think ourselves perfect. In humility is found perseverance toward the Good.

Divine warfare is founded within the paradox of human nature. A war unto which one side has already always won. As such. any fight towards and into the darkness is only an airless descent into confusion. How can one act in accordance with that which is without any definition? The abyss is limitless and endless, and abounds in such a place one may lose their soul. The pain of such a descent will not bring about a feeling of depth nor fear of hitting some floor. For all that shall come from acceptance of darkness will be true death, and within that, a yearning for the unity of their True Nature (their soul) which one forgave for the sake of a few worldly trinkets.

Imagine, if you will, what it truly is to act in accordance with the confusion of the dark and the malevolence of sin. It can only be becoming a slave to the promise of an answer to a question already solved. A life spent in befuddlement and loss, going here and there searching for whatever may fill the pitch-black for that fleeting moment. But sin and darkness as all-encompassing nothingness merely subsume and disappear all which is subsumed into it. To move away from the Light, and continue going, is to be eternally lost with no hope of closure. So it is that one can now see that from within such a tyrannical realm of darkness, even the smallest of flames would shine ever bright! Think of such a sight and feeling—days, weeks, months, or even a lifetime trapped within this expanse of torturous uncertainty, that a gentle light flickers or rises from somewhere finally defined! Would one not run? Would one not stride from behind thankful tears to kneel beneath this light?

Will

Human will

Following on from this need to be aware of ourselves and our inner contradictions is a much-needed discussion on will, both ours and God's. Let us begin where we can, with ourselves. If we are to act a certain way, then it certainly makes sense to question to what extent we can act, and what it is we are acting for. The will, our will, is that faculty that allows us a free choice between different particulars offered to us. Will we give some money to the homeless or just pass it by? Will we stick to our fast or decide we need to eat a large, gluttonous meal? Will we follow our own lower desires or aim for something higher? It is just that faculty which allows us to choose and select via the light of reason. I believe there has yet to be a greater articulation of will, and will in relation to the soul, than that from Plato's *Phaedrus* (2005), often known as the *Phaedrus Chariot* or the Allegory of the Chariot

> We will liken the soul to the composite nature of a pair of winged horses and a charioteer. Now the horses and charioteers of the gods are all good and of good descent, but those of other races are mixed; and first the charioteer of the human soul drives a pair,

and secondly one of the horses is noble and of noble breed, but the other quite the opposite in breed and character. Therefore in our case driving is necessarily difficult and troublesome.

Our soul is two horses then, one noble and white and one wayward and black, the former with an appetite for the transcendent (God) and the latter with an appetite for the carnal (and ultimately non-rational) desires. Put simply, it is our task as the charioteer to keep control of these horses. When one first looks at this allegory, however, it appears that the only task should be to strictly adhere to the path of the white horse, ignoring the black altogether. For why would we ever want anything to do with that horse which seeks to drag us down, away from God, towards hell? But we need to understand that these allegorical horses are not simply *within* us in some relative sense, but that this splitting between the Lord and the world is that rift we feel in our conscience at all times.

So it cannot be, if we are to remain with the allegory, that we disregard and let loose one horse for the other in some-or-other act of insane severance. For as I have shown, man's infallibility *is* within his very being, man *has fallen*, and so there shall never be a case wherein we have one horse and not the other. Further on Plato makes it clear

> when perfect and fully winged she (the chariot) soars upward, and orders the whole world; whereas the imperfect soul, losing her wings and drooping in her flight at last settles on the solid ground.

And so it is that if the charioteer (ourselves) cannot successfully pilot the chariot upwards, then the wings of *both* horses shall wither away and we shall be led downwards. Viewed via a Christian lens this places us in a peculiar, but ultimately correct, position. As one can see it takes *both* horses to pull the chariot upwards towards the heavens, and, strangely, only takes the acts and pull of the black horse to wither the wings of both and send us astray. Moving forward in our own lives it is therefore not the case that we shall ever be without that carnal, lower horse. It is of us, and part of us, as much as the heavenly-directed horse. Man's position is not of a rock which is fully material (lower), nor that of an angel being fully divine (above), Man's position is of mediation, and his will is the faculty which chooses between these two states and conclusions of being. Ultimately, the individual human will have but one choice, heaven or hell.

But where does this, practically speaking, leave us? It is clear now that we cannot commit the error of someone such as Origen, a 2nd-century Christian ascetic who sought out a physician to castrate him, therein in allegorically cutting away the black horse. Origen didn't succeed in his endeavour, yet this tale outlines our reality as individuals trying to do good here on earth, in that we *do* have the propensity to commit evil and ignore the Good, and that choice will never leave until the day we die. That black, carnal, and wayward horse not only shall always remain with us but is very much needed for our ascent to the heavens. That wayward stallion is with us for life, a part of ourselves we perhaps wish was not, and how do we often treat it in the knowledge that it is the encapsulation of our base and carnal desires? Do we not beat and berate that horse? Do we not try, during any of its attempts to beckon its head, to simply yell at it in dismay? Even though we know that its actions are born solely from our own fallen hearts.

Dare I say this as a course of action—be kind to the wayward horse, for he knows not what he does. I am *not* declaring that one should excuse that horse, not allow his nature to go unchecked, but in attending to this allegory in a Christian manner, we must be ready to forgive. To forgive the wayward horse of others as we forgive our own. Yet as no one learned anything of themselves from a point of ignorance or drowning out the noise, so too we must have the courage to turn to this horse, this part of ourselves, and *accept* that it is we who commit these wrongful actions and no other, and therein learn from them. It is in the taming of the wayward horse that the ascent to heaven can truly begin. As one does not plant vegetables in a garden full of weeds, so too will a closer relationship with God be more difficult if we have put no effort towards witnessing and correcting our own mistakes. If we merely *excuse* and justify the actions of the wayward horse to everything else but ourselves then he shall never learn. If he yelps or pulls, drags or moans, we must know that these actions come not from some external pressure, but from ourselves giving ourselves over to the easy and the comfortable, foregoing courage and the bearing of our Cross for the sake—once again—of a few fickle worldly things. That poor horse, born from our fallen root and blamed equally for its actions.

It is by slowly, slowly dragging up these weeds and taming this horse that we can find a point of harmony and mediation, allowing the aforementioned clearance of darkness thus opening the way for light. The temperament and desires of that horse must be looked upon from a position of silence and honesty, for no other made them but ourselves. We may find in time that there is that which the horse seeks time and time again, that it has favourite desires which seem to rule over all reason, and the why of these desires is often placed in a far different place than we ever imagined. Perhaps we feel we have been doing an okay job in taming this horse, and progressing nicely. Yet our kindness and attentiveness towards this black beast must be merciless, we must nourish, love, and guide it with a determined fervour. For as the Lord says (Revelation 3:16):

> *But because thou art lukewarm, and neither cold, not hot, I will begin to vomit thee out of my mouth.*

Is it enough to make the same excuses all shall make time and time again, entering into that lukewarm life, destined to be spat out? We may declare we have done as much as we could, tried as we might, but this declaration would likely be from the position of someone who has justified to themselves why there could have been no other path. No, I say we must arise and tend to our wayward horse in all hours, sharing with it all our errors, explaining to it where we are both going wrong. For if it is not tamed, none of us shall make it. You know not what you do, and neither do I, but I know what I must try to do.

I have spoken little of the white and noble horse, and possibly now you can see why that is. Of what use would it be at this juncture to expand upon the lightness of that path the white horse shall open if we are still grinning alongside our wayward friend? We need to tackle the root of darkness without mercy, and in doing so allow those false wayward guides a glimpse of the light. One may in time sit within the chariot and witness a harmony with black tamed to white, witnessing the darkness dispel, evil fall away, and a transparent obedience come forth and lead us upward! But not if we do not act with humility and kindness towards others and ourselves. Carry with your thought and feeling of the eternal into the finite, of the immortal into the mortal, of light into dark, and therein there shall be no sense in the latter at all. To arrive at the point where many small missteps of the wayward have been revealed in the light, and in clarity of sight, with eyes that can see, we wonder why at all we ever bothered with the other path.

To truly tame this black beast, then, is not a matter of tugging at the reins in acts of prayer that almost rupture the veins in one's head, but a slow, quiet task of revealing to ourselves how full of folly and nothingness that 'other' path is. 'Look, dear wayward steed, there is nothing on this path, why are we still going this way?' To reveal the irrationality and thus neuter the desire altogether, 'all those things you head towards will one day be gone, lost completely to time, let me help you understand'. I have never liked, in such cases as these, to leave the reader without a clear example of just what it is I am on about. An example has as its hidden backdrop the knowledge of the afterlife, and of Christ's revelation to man.

What one of us has not sought at some-or-other time in our lives a particular material thing? Be it a car, a house, a big TV, or a qualification, I imagine we have all quite desperately *wanted* such a thing. Think back to when you were a child, and how you possibly found it so difficult to sleep before Christmas day in excitement of the presents you may receive. Now, a more important task, think back—if you can—to all those things you once wanted in life which you didn't receive or acquire. What happened? What has happened since then … anything? I imagine your life turned out not so different, if at all, from the lack of this item. And this is how it is with all finite things, all worldly things. For could any such thing even be in comparison to the life of the noble horse and where he seeks to lead us? It is not that I wish to be no longer interested in this-or-that thing in favour of another *thing*, but that we yearn for another language, another Kingdom, altogether!

We began here with the will, with an individual's—*yours and mine*—human will. The faculty which allows us choice, gives us agency. I stated that there is only one choice and it is between heaven and hell. But in truth, this choice bears a grander weight, for *there is only a single choice*, and it is between God and nothing. And that is why we must be kind to the wayward horse in ourselves, for he knows not as we know not, and the more we come to internalise that all which is sought for along the wayward path will amount to *nothing*, the more we shall prepare ourselves to be able to grow closer to God.

God's Will

Of course, we do need to speak of that other white and noble horse, and, most importantly, we need to talk about where it is leading us. Allegorically speaking, for the Christian, the white horse is first leading us *to* God's Will, and therein helping us to simply follow God's Will.

Put plainly, we can know that God's Will is the path that will lead us to greater holiness, to further spiritual growth, and therefore lead us closer to Him in general. It is a tricky thing to write of God's Will because one doesn't wish to determine exactly just what it is. Yet this in itself brings us back around to a discussion of our own obliviousness once more.

It is a common question for both the convert and lifelong Christian alike—Just what does God want from me? What does He want me to do? It appears at first glance that if this query had a clear answer, or perhaps a clear list of answers such as Go to College, Go to University, Become a Monk, Become a priest, Marry person X, etc. then life would be so much simpler. But in much the same light as what it means to love someone, so too would such direct answers to our existential and theological questions negate the possibility of faith altogether. If we knew just exactly what God expected from us down to the last detail, our choices would not be made from faith, but from a nonsensical divine checklist. But as we all understand some decisions we considered correct failed, that which we at first ignored may have become a large part of our lives, and throughout all our days are small moments of spontaneity and surprise that test our covenant with the Lord.

This Will of God's though, just what is it? Though it is that which brings us closer to Him, it can also be that we make decisions of our own volition that bring us closer to Him too. And so what is it to decide between two options, one of which is more in alignment with God's own will? This is called *discernment*. In his *Sermon on Love* (2007) St Augustine tells us to 'Love God and do what you will', and to modern ears this might sound like just the passage of Tradition we've been looking for, one which seemingly justifies any actions as fine as long as we love God. Of course, this is not what is meant by this passage.

To love God, as we have seen, is to love both Creator and His creation. Ergo to 'love God' is to love, and as it stands there is much that man may himself will that is certainly not undertaken from a place of love. So it is that doing what one will be aligned with the previous section on human nature, in loving God *and then* doing what one will, it is such that we must make the noble horse our priority, taming the wayward horse *in light* of the noble horse's passage towards the Lord. If we are to love God and His Creation prior to our own acts of willingness it should not be that we shall go astray. It is only when we reverse the quote by St Augustine and go about our own affairs first and love God after the fact that we lose our footing.

Faith, grace, love, and will, are a rough passage towards making decisions pleasing to the Lord. Yet still, even at this thoroughly grounded juncture, we appear to still be none the wiser to just what it is that is to come forth and guide our lives. Even once the roots of faith and love have been planted deep in a garden slowly being stripped of weeds we still remain uncertain as to the 'what' of God's Will. With such matters of ambiguity, however, we mustn't forget the certain foundations we may turn to as a guide toward the Spirit. We may lose ourselves so deeply in the belief that we do not and can not know, that by a prideful shadow of our own making, we occlude the simplicity of Scripture and tradition that is at hand at all times.

We have the Old Testament prophets Abraham, Moses, and Elijah to guide us through to revelation of Christ, the tales and teachings from the Life of Jesus Christ, we have the apostolic tradition settling the institution of the Church, and finally, we have the lives of the Saints, all of which contains such a spiritual wealth of *Right and Just* knowledge that one could not hope to even scratch the surface in their lifetime. In trying to get closer to God we cannot go wrong by learning from those who have already done so, priests, monastics, Saints, and Apostles are our guides in these matters. This does not mean that we should act solely in imitation (except of Christ Himself ... if we can), for imitating those we read of would be to do outside of various contexts, leading us once more away from the reality of our world and our own wayward horse towards an ideal that cannot be sustained.

I would like to take a detour here, a much-needed digression on something I shall call the 'Saintly ideal', that from here on I shall just call the 'ideal'. I feel that not only is this needed in relation to our current discussion of the interplay between our own will and God's, but also because it is emphatically one of the greatest errors many Christians (especially new, vitally zealous converts) make when approaching their spiritual life. When we set out in life with the task of being a Good Christian we may quickly find a priest we admire, a parishioner whose life inspires us, or even a Saint we seek to unknowingly, literally imitate. We may create from our reading and experience with these people or writings an ideal Christian self within us that we from now on hastily seek to replicate within the world. Be it saying various long prayers, extensively studying long theological tracts, or even undertaking ascetic practices, we will find that we now have some other life to upkeep. But the time *will* come when we can no longer upkeep this life. We will find ourselves mumbling our prayers, burning out on pious literature, and maybe even making ourselves quite unwell via asceticism. Why is this? Why does this strict imitation not work? Because we are trying to be someone who God did not create us to be. By its very definition, this ideal Christian self is not our real Christian self because it simply isn't us.

We've created an ideal image of what a Christian is to be whilst overlooking our own self, our own fallen nature, and our own life. We will find that we have attempted to take on the chariot piloting of another person altogether, and from this position, both our failures and successes will make no sense because they weren't meant for us and have been stripped from the context. And so in beginning with the certainties mentioned prior, we also have to begin with the first certainty we have in this world, ourselves. From this position of the ideal we fail at being someone we never were in the first place and then feel ourselves detached from God in the process. We feel as if His forgiveness and love are only relevant if we live up to this fluxing ideal we have created. This is objectively false, and—new converts especially—need to understand that God's love, as unconditional and freely given, is for ourselves *as we are*, for we are God's children and we must begin from *this* position and not elsewhere. God's love and forgiveness are for *you*, not the 'you' one believes they *should* be.

In returning to the discussion on God's Will we now have two certain foundations as a means to find out just what exactly it is, namely, Scripture and tradition, and ourselves (complete with all our faults and oversights). If we are honest about who we are, what we do and do not do, and our understanding of Christ's teaching we shall slowly begin to see how certain choices pull us this way and that, which decisions we often fall prey to, and what it is *we* need to do.

And when we settle into this humble and honest way of living we will soon be able to clearly see the fruits of the Lord, be they big or small, cast forth in their righteous light. The process itself shall become the fruits, full of peace and joy, of an acceptance that allows us to love more fully. But what of those moments of strife, anxiety, anguish, pain, and desire? Where we have given ourselves over as much as we feel we can and still life seems to be dealing us a bad hand? In these moments we must attempt to keep our eyes fixed on Christ, on the heavenly Kingdom. The darkness and temptation of the world shall be until the day we are no longer of that self-same world, the Lord's promise is of another Kingdom, of another joy, and of another peace entirely. A feeling that grows within the heart and lends transcendent courage against the suffering of the world.

Do not give yourself over to the false mentality of the world that promises closure and completion in all things. For if you are attempting to 'work out' God's Will then you are silently stating that in time you will be His equal. We do not even know ourselves, this much is clear by taking a quick glance at the world, and yet we constantly seek to fully know God. He knows you better than you ever will for He created you. Be patient, humble, open, determined, and loving. Most of all … persevere. Your faith is not guaranteed. Recall the feeling of God's love as much as possible, recall moments when you fell into His embrace, remember his gentle guidance, and keep it in mind for when the darkness once more raises its head.

Submitting our will to the Lord

But as always questions still remain, and here we find another that the everyday Christians will ask themselves time and time again: How can I submit myself to God? Or in relation to what we've been talking about here: How can I submit myself to the *Will* of God? Now, many people who are new to the faith find such language a little off-putting. Submission, obedience, or even *slavery!* Aren't these terms for one who has simply given over their personal agency and responsibility to something else as a means to possibly avoid it? Actually, no. Quite the opposite in fact. As I've already made clear in a couple of sections, there's no such thing as non-sacrifice. Life is sacrifice (whether you're a Christian or not). In deciding to have, hold, or direct ourselves towards one thing, it's more often the case that in doing so we move away from something else. We cannot eat our cake and have it too. Life is a matter of preferences and our personal selections are always a question regarding where our real valuation lies.

It seems so severe to be a slave to Christ or a slave to God's Will. And yet, what are our other options? If we do not follow the Lord then we follow the world, and would one rather be a slave to charity of greed? Love or hate? Justice or vengeance? Hope or despair? I'd like to think that the majority of people wouldn't think twice about selecting the former in all cases, for if one were to choose the latter they would in truth burn themselves up quite quickly. So when we submit ourselves to God it is a matter of selection, as with all things. The difference is that in choosing God over other things we may very well be (and will likely be) choosing the more difficult option. We may choose to fast instead of eat, to think of others before ourselves, or to suffer instead of ignore. In this sense perhaps it becomes a little easier to see what submitting our own wills to God looks like in a practical sense and why it might be a bit more difficult than we first thought.

For it is most emphatically the peculiar question regarding the popularity of religion in the world: Why—if there are so many devoutly religious people who abide by a plethora of good teachings—is there still so much hatred, greed, and selfishness in the world? The answer isn't difficult. The answer is because we're fallen, and from our fallen nature we succumb to the temptations of the world and find ourselves straying from God. It is easy to act in the manner of a fallen, sinful creature because *we are* fallen, sinful creatures. And it's from this position that when we look back at the idea of the 'Saintly ideal' I posited earlier, we see how creating such a false version of ourselves (this ideal self possibly even being not fallen) can lead us to a lot of personal, inner harm. What, then, do we practically need to do to even begin aligning our will with God's? We need to be honest.

In trying to align ourselves with God's Will, what, in truth, are we attempting to do? We are attempting to receive His grace. We are trying to comport ourselves in a certain open, humble manner to accept grace. Yet grace and faith in their interconnection are in part a choice, and therein must begin to be accepted from one of the most difficult moments of honesty, the admittance of the *need* for God.

Let us think back to those Christmas presents we never received, and thought so much of at the time, and yet their absence changed nothing. This is how *we* often see God's Will. Being humans and prey to folly and temptation we think we know better than God, and we find ourselves praying for this-or-that thing whatever it may be, not stopping to ponder on whether or not we're trying to shoehorn our own will into God's. Before all our desires, wants, and supposed requirements within this world we need to find it in ourselves to ask God for one thing, *Himself*. If we find this too dishonest in the sense that we still feel our hearts panging for something worldly then we can ask God to take away this desire. To be as honest as one can be is to see oneself as clearly as one can. To repeatedly return to our own minds, habits, and actions, bringing them before God in our hearts and making it clear to Him just how we are. Of course, He already knows just how we are, for He created us. And yet in this act of returning to God over and over, of bringing our faults before him (whether in Confession or private prayer) we continually try to sincerely see ourselves as how we are and not how we'd *like* to be.

* * *

Exercise 10

Before undertaking this walk sit for a few minutes and quiet your thoughts.

You've come a long way and hopefully, understand your own relationship with God a little bit better. This exercise, then, is simply a repetition of the first exercise, this time without any guidelines.

Say a single prayer.

* * *

The afterlife, salvation, and a possible conclusion

Considering the non-dogmatic approach I've at least attempted to undertake throughout this book, this (non) conclusion was the most difficult. At first, I wrote another section on hell, purgatory, and heaven. I then tried to draw that all together with a discussion regarding salvation and what it is to 'be saved'. I quickly found myself, however, sounding much like those people who drew me away from the spirit at such a young age. Those who were quick to judge and damn others to hell, in spite of the fact all they were doing all day was, well, judging and damning. The strictly aesthetic and visualised versions of the afterlife do little more than bolster the world in various directions. Many imagine hell as the most niche of punishments for their worst enemy from some sort of retributive position of personal justice. Many imagine heaven as an extension of their worldly life here on earth, except, forever and infinitely better.

After the pace of this book, it felt entirely anathema to my understanding of the spirit to begin stating that one *must* do this or that to avoid some-or-other agony I know nothing about in any certain sense. Even to proclaim haste in terms of saving oneself appears to be little more than trying to get someone on one's side, as opposed to actually caring about their life and their troubles. It's for this reason I feel that many priests dislike the word *obligation* when it comes to Sunday Mass or service. Even though, theologically speaking, it may very well be an obligation to go to Mass as a practising Christian, attending on Sundays solely because it's what one feels they *must* do misses the point altogether. If we are to revert back to the basics of this book, which is to say, grace and love, then in truth no action performed under the weight of guilt, obligation, or fear can be fully spiritual.

If we feel guilty about who we are in light of God's love, it might be the case that we undertake actions for the sake of trying to save spiritual face, trying to give back because 'That's what is done', as opposed to doing so out of a genuine, heartfelt desire. Equally, if we attend church due to an obligation then our faith has become little more than a quantified gesture, an attempt to gain qualitative favour via quantitative means. Finally, if we perform certain acts only because we are terrified of what comes next, then it may very well be the case that deep down we haven't changed at all, but are expending a lot of energy trying to adhere to a 'Saintly ideal' that is far from who we are.

We are told to imitate Christ, this is true. *'Whoever says he abides in him ought to walk in the same way in which he walked'* (1 John 2:6), yet it is equally true that we are told to imitate Him and not others' imitations of Him which so often happens. Our journey through life is solely our own, this goes without saying. Yet, when it comes to our own salvation—an idea that has been thoroughly damaged by the image of town crier types yelling 'Save yourselves!' from a street corner—we are quick to look elsewhere as to what it is we should be doing. We are quick to try to imitate those we consider to be good as to try to become good ourselves. Our acts and our salvation, however, are ours alone, and trying to contort the context of anyone else onto our own life will only beget confusion.

Am I saying to not worry about where we go when we die? In a sense, yes. But only because I think specifically *worrying* about tends to alter one's focus to that of hastily making amends as opposed to just living the best one can. Your relationship with heaven and hell—however one wishes to understand them—is also yours alone, and no other can truly speak of your heart. This often-panicked relationship with salvation brings us back to the introduction of this book, to the common approach regarding the Trinity. In thinking of salvation as some far-off act or *event* unto which we are meriting points, we may be quick to leap to the Father, reading His words plainly as a means to somehow objectively acquire our merit. As it is, we are each individual human beings amidst our own subjectivities and contexts, and a quick leap to the Father before journeying with the Spirit and the Son is a passage of ignorance. Yes, there is objective truth, and no, we shall not acquire it in full. Subjectivity, our own appreciation, and contextual attempt at imitating Christ is not incorrect, but simply a smaller part of a relationship with the objective, it's all we have and it's ours to use.

We have the time we find ourselves in. We have the lives we find ourselves living, the family and friends we find ourselves keeping, and we have the actions we find ourselves deciding between. Personally, I have found little to no use in fantasising about some far-off religious utopia, or politicalism that will get everyone in line and make the world a better place. More often than not, those who loudly proclaim others to be bad are doing so as an excuse to avoid doing good. Likewise, it's often the case that the evil gets an overabundance of airtime both because of its theatrics, but also because goodness tends to be quiet.

Don't get anxious, then, when you look at your own life and believe yourself to be lacking. You are as God, the Absolute, the Found of all Being made you, and, *as you are* have a purpose and meaning, here and now.

* * *

I hope this book has gone some way in at least opening Christianity for you.

BIBLIOGRAPHY

Catechism of the Catholic Church. 1995. 2nd ed. New York: Doubleday.
Couliano, Ioan P. 1988. *Eros and Magic in the Renaissance*. London: University of Chicago Press.
Eckhart, Meister. 2009. *The Complete Mystical Works of Meister Eckhart*. Maurice O'C Walshe (Trans.). New York: Herder & Herder Book, The Crossroad Publishing Company. (Paraphrase of his *Speech 5b DW I + Speech 30 DW II + On Detachment DW V*)
Lewis, C.S. (1940) 2012. *The Problem of Pain*. London: Collins.
Wallace, David Foster. 2009. *This Is Water*. New York: Little, Brown.
Henry, John. 2022. *Discourses Addressed to Mixed Congregations*. Paderborn: Salzwasser-Verlag.
Thomas, Aquinas Saint. 2018. *Summa Theologica Complete in a Single Volume*. Claremont: Coyote Canyon Press.
Pieper, Josef. 2009. *Leisure: The Basis of Culture; the Philosophical Act*. San Francisco: Ignatius Press.
Plato. 2005. *Phaedrus*. C. J. Rowe (Trans.). London; New York: Penguin Books.
Saint Augustine. 2007. *Sermon on Love*. In Daniel Edward Doyle and Edmund Hill. *Essential Sermons*. Hyde Park, NY: New City Press.

INDEX

'Absolute', 10
   worldview, 7
afterlife, 69
   Allegory of Long Spoons, 73
   'beatific vision', 70
   death, 70
   heaven, 69, 70–71
   hell, 69, 73–75
   purgatory, 69, 71–73
   reality of hell, 74
   reflections on hell and eternal
      separation, 75
   reflective meditation, 75–76
   spiritual fire, 72
   three forms of, 69
Allegory. *See also* afterlife
   of Long Spoons, 73
   of the Chariot, 147–148
alternative spiritual currents, 18–20
annunciation to Joseph, 38–39
Anointing of the Sick, 64
Apostles, 64

Augustine, Saint, 152
awakening to divine purpose, 38–39

Baptism, 61, 123
   and self-reflection, 123–127
'beatific vision', 70. *See also* afterlife
Beatitudes, the, 50, 109
   Kingdom of Heaven, 51
   meek, 51, 52
   mercy, 55
   reflective journey through, 56
Bethlehem and Star, 41
'Bible, the', 31, 37
   'Gospels, the', 36
   'human fingerprint', 35
   New Testament, 35–36
   Old Testament, 36

charity, 136–140. *See also* rich and poor
Christ, 7, 20, 29. *See also* Christ, life of
   Peter's denial of, 92–93
   radical wisdom of, 50–56

166 INDEX

recruiting disciples, 47–49
and rich young man, 131–133
temptation in desert, 43–47, 143
Christian
   Baptism, 123
   generic birth, 123
   morality, 144
   path of, 79
   second birth, 123
   themes, 79
   true sacrifice and love, 136–140
   values, 14, 15
Christianity, 7, 29
   'Bible, the', 31
   Christ, 29
   journey of discovery, 29–33
   materialist understanding of, 22
   in modern world, 7–12
   reflecting on religious education and beliefs, 33
Christianity misconceptions, 21
   finding connection through prayer, 24–26
   finding God through experience, 28
   'God', 22–24
   beyond intellectual assent, 28
   journey beyond doubt and confusion, 27–28
   language limitations in understanding divine, 22–24
   materialist understanding of Christianity, 22
   misconceptions of God, 24–26
   modern education, 21–22
   prayerful bridge, 27–28
Christ, life of, 37
   awakening to divine purpose, 38–39
   Beatitudes, the, 50–56
   choosing and being chosen, 47–49
   connecting with world around you, 49–50
   consciousness and spiritual potential, 40
   contemplative walking, 49–50
   Cross, the, 41–43

Gospel of Matthew, 37–38
Great Chain of Being, 39–40
human nature and compassion, 56
Jesus recruiting disciples, 47–49
Jesus' temptation in desert, 43–47
'justice', 54
metanoia, 53
'Passion, the', 56
radical wisdom of Jesus, 50–56
reflections on calling of Twelve Disciples, 47–49
role of friction in temptation and faith, 45
sceptre, 41
Sermon on the Mount, 50–56
spiritual mourning, 52–54
symbolic significance of Bethlehem and Star, 41
symbolism in annunciation to Joseph, 38–39
'Temptation of Jesus, The', 43–47
'wake/rise up', 40
Confession, 63
Confirmation, 62
consciousness and spiritual potential, 40
contemplative walking, 49–50
Couliano, Ioan P., 16
Cross, the, 41–43
Crucifixion, 57

darkness, 117, 142. *See also* light and darkness
death, 70. *See also* afterlife
   avoidance of, 11–12
denial of Jesus, Peter's, 92–93
discernment, 152
discipleship, 125
discursive meditation, 95
divine warfare, 146
dogmatism, 18
dual nature of humanity, 148

Eckhart, Meister, 52
Eden, 58
Eucharist, 61, 62

evil, 116
Extreme Unction, 64

faith, 97. *See also* nihilism to faith
   choice of, 99–101
   depths of, 106–107
   divine invitation, 99–101
   grace and, 87
   and individual, 8–9
   leap of faith, 101
   misconceptions, 98
   negative discursive meditation, 106–107
   nurturing faith, 102–106
   overcoming doubt, 105–106
   path of, 97–99
   profession of, 100
   role of friction in temptation and, 45
   silence and honest faith, 111–113

generic birth, 123
God, misconceptions of, 24–26
God's
   law, 10
   love, 89
   term, 22–24
   will, 151–155
'Gospels, the', 36
   John, 93
   Luke, 116, 125
   Matthew, 37–38, 40, 50, 143
grace, 79, 99
   actual grace, 80, 81
   divine gift, 79–82, 85–87
   and faith, 87
   feeling, 85–87
   foundation of, 82–85
   journey of grace and love, 159–161
   path to salvation, 79–82
   Peace Prayer, 87–88
   prayer of selflessness, 87–88
   Prayer of St Francis, 87–88
   sanctifying, 80, 81
   separate forms of, 80
   state of sin, 85
   surrendering to divine grace, 87–88

   true nature of spiritual slavery, 84–85
   within us, 126
Great Chain of Being, 39–40
grow, 121

heaven, 69, 70–71. *See also* afterlife
hell, 69, 73–75. *See also* afterlife
Henry, John, 102
Holy Orders, Sacrament of, 64
human
   frailty and sinfulness, 144–145
   paradox, 144–146
   will, 147–151
humanity dual nature of, 148
humility and silence, 109
   art of silence, 118–120
   clearing corridor of soul, 109–111
   corridor of silence, 114–118
   darkness and light, 117
   from innocence to worldly noise, 114–115
   journey towards God, 118–120
   noise and modernity, 114–118, 119
   path to silence and honest faith, 111–113
   path to spiritual poverty, 109–113
   silence, 118
   spiritual innocence and overcoming noise, 114–118
   weeklong meditation journey, 120

ideal Christian self, 153–154
inner kingdom, 125–126
institutional Christianity, 17

Jesus. *See* Christ
'justice', 54

Kingdom of Heaven, 51

Lewis, C. S., 74
light, 117
   symbolism of, 141–144
light and darkness, 141
   Christian morality, 144

Christ's temptation in
    wilderness, 143
darkness, 142
divine warfare, 146
human frailty and sinfulness,
    144–145
human paradox, 144–146
illumination, choice, and spiritual
    warfare, 141–144
light and love, 141–144
to sin, 146
spiritual battle, 143, 144–146
struggle between, 144–146
symbolism of light, 141–144
Lord's Prayer, 27
love, 89
    contemplative journey, 95
    discursive meditation, 95
    divine essence, 91–94
    over dogma, 18–20
    essence of, 89–91
    exploring through meditation, 95
    God's love, 89
    journey of grace and, 159–161
    light and, 141–144
    unconditional love, 91–94

Matrimony, Sacrament of, 64
meditation
    journey, 120
    reflective, 75–76
meek, 51, 52
mercy, 55
metanoia, 53
modern world, 7
moral virtues, 144
mourning, spiritual, 52–54
myth of progress, 8

New Man, 123–127
New Testament, 35–36
nihilism to faith, 3. *See also* faith
    alternative spiritual currents, 18–20
    avoidance of death, 11–12
    Christianity in modern world, 7–12
    Christian values, 14, 15

degradation of sacred, 16–18
faith and individual, 8–9
illusion of intellectual superiority,
    4–5
institutional Christianity, 17
loss of spiritual depth in modern
    Christianity, 16–18
love over dogma, 18–20
myth of progress, 8
'open prayer', 5
paradox of modern freedom, 9–10
path of grace, 5–6
pseudo-religious education, 3–4
reconciling Christian virtues with
    modern values, 12–16
reformation, sacred, and Couliano,
    16–18
soul in modern world, 12–16
soul's struggle, 12–16
spiritual exploration, 5
spiritual roots of modern
    morality, 13
noise, 114–118, 119

Offering, Widow's, The, 136. *See also* rich
    and poor
Old Testament, 36
    prophets, 153
'open prayer', 5
Origen, 149
Original Sin, 58, 135

Parable of the Sower, 122
paradox of modern freedom, 9–10
Passion, 58
Passion, The, 56, 57, 59
    Christ's Crucifixion, 57
    impact of Christ's resurrection, 59
    foundation of Sacraments, 59
    profound redemption, 58
Path
    of Christian, 79
    of Grace, 5–6
    of Submission, 155–157
'peacemaker', 55
Peace Prayer, 87–88

INDEX

Penance/Confession, 63
Peter's denial of Jesus, 92–93
Phaedrus, 147
Pieper, Josef, 118–119
Plato, 147, 148
'poor widow', 136–137. *See also* rich and poor
poverty, 134–136. *See also* rich and poor
    spiritual, 109–113
prayer
    Lord's, 27
    open, 5
    of selflessness, 87–88
    of St Francis, 87–88
pride, 135
pure heart, 55
purgatory, 69, 71–73. *See also* afterlife

reflections
    on calling of Twelve Disciples, 47–49
    on hell and eternal separation, 75
    on religious education and beliefs, 33
rich and poor, 131
    charity, 136–140
    lessons from story of rich young man, 131–133
    moral tightrope, 134–136
    Original Sin, 135
    'poor widow', 136–137
    poverty, 134–136
    pride, 135
    true sacrifice and love in Christian virtue, 136–140
    types of treasure, 133
    understanding wealth and poverty, 131–133
    Widow's Offering, The, 136
roots of modern morality, spiritual, 13

Sacrament(s), 59, 61–64
    Baptism, 61
    Confirmation, 62
    Eucharist, 62
    of Extreme Unction or Anointing of the Sick, 64
    of Holy Orders, 64
    of Matrimony, 64
    Penance/Confession, 63
    sacred, 16–18
Saint Augustine, 152
'Saintly ideal', 153, 156, 160
salvation, 159–161
Satan, 116
sceptre, 41
second birth, 123
self, ideal Christian, 153–154
selflessness, prayer of, 87–88
self-reflection, Baptism and, 123–127
self-transformation, 126–127
self-understanding, 151–155
Sermon on the Mount, 50–56, 109
silence, 114–118, 118–120
soul, 65
    body and soul in Christian belief, 66
    chariot of, 148
    cultivating, 121–123
    humanity, 65–66
    in modern world, 12–16
    role in redemption, 66–67
    saving one's soul, 65
spiritual
    alternative currents, 18–20
    mourning, 52–54
    potential and consciousness, 40
    poverty, 109–113
    roots of modern morality, 13
    warfare, 144–146
spiritual growth, 121. *See also* afterlife
    battle, 143
    challenge of true discipleship, 125
    cultivating the soul, 121–123
    discovering inner kingdom, 125–126
    divine guidance on path to, 126–127
    fire, 72
    gardener's approach to, 121–123
    grace within us, 126
    grow, 121
    intersection of material and spiritual realms, 127–129

journey towards self-
transformation, 126–127
living in tension, 127–129
New Man, 123–127
our potential as Christian, 127–129
Parable of the Sower, 122
reflections on Luke 17:21, 125–126
transformative power of Baptism
and self-reflection, 123–127
Star and Bethlehem, 41
state of sin, 85
Sunday Mass or service, 160
symbolism
in annunciation to Joseph, 38–39
Bethlehem and Star, 41
of light, 141–144

'Temptation of Jesus, The', 43–47
Testament, 36
Thomas, Aquinas Saint, 112
treasure types, 133. *See also* rich
and poor
Trinity, ix–x
Twelve Disciples, 47–49

vision, beatific, 70

'wake/rise up', 40
Wallace, David Foster, 84
warfare, spiritual, 144–146
wealth and poverty. *See* rich and poor
Widow's Offering, The, 136. *See also* rich
and poor
will, 147
aligning God's will with, 155–157
Allegory of the Chariot, 147–148
chariot of soul, 148
discernment, 152
discernment and self-
understanding, 151–155
dual nature of humanity, 148
God's will, 151–155
human will, 147–151
ideal Christian self, 153–154
journey towards God, 147–151
path of submission, 155–157
'Saintly ideal', 153, 156
silent reflection and prayer, 157
submitting our will to the lord,
155–157
taming of the wayward horse,
147–151
worldview, absolute, 7